Thou Shalt Not Be an Indian

A Residential School Survivor's Story

by Robert Kakakaway

THOU SHALT NOT BE AN INDIAN
A Residential School Survivor's Story

Copyright© 2020 Robert Kakakaway
511 Sandy Ridge Place
Whitecap, SK. S7K 2L2
Email: kakakaway@sasktel.net
Website: www.kakakaway.com

All rights reserved. No part of this book may be reproduced in any form by any electronic or mechanical means. This includes information storage and retrieval systems, without permission in writing from the publisher, except by a reviewer who may quote brief passages in a review. Any resemblance to persons living or dead should be apparent to them, especially if the author has been kind enough to have provided their real names. All events described herein actually happened, though on occasion the author has taken certain, very small, liberties with chronology because that is his right as a First Nation – Residential School survivor.

Editing by Lisa Binion, Lisa's Writopia Editing Services

Published in Canada 2020

Acknowledgements

First of all, I give thanks to our Creator for guiding me through this difficult childhood. I acknowledge my siblings, cousins, friends, and all the students who attended Marieval Indian Residential School. May you find comfort in knowing your story is being told.

I acknowledge my wife, Vanessa who supported me as I wrote about my experiences at Marieval. Writing about the painful memories of my childhood was a difficult thing to do. There were times when I stopped writing, put my head on my desk and cried.

I returned to visit the school many years later. As I walked around "The Block" I pointed out the different classrooms to my wife. Those painful memories came flooding back, and I dropped to my knees. I cried for my brothers, cousins and friends who attended this school and passed away thinking it was wrong to be an Indian.

I acknowledge my editor, Lisa Binion from Lisa's Writopia Editing Services, in Beattyville, Kentucky. I also give a big thank you to Jason EagleSpeaker for his assistance in publishing my book.

To my wife, Vanessa and my children (including the ones, I've been blamed for.) I dedicate my book to the students who attended Marieval Indian Residential School.

Prologue

I heard your cries for help as they pulled you away from your family. The long nights in the dorm were lonely times as you cried yourself to sleep. You would stay awake for hours wondering why you couldn't go home. You often thought about going home, but the days at the "Mission" turned into weeks, the weeks into months, and the months into years.

As time passed, your parents and grandparents became strangers. You couldn't understand what they were saying when they spoke your language. You forgot the old stories your grandparents told you as a child. You no longer had the urge to dance at pow-wows; instead, you felt shy and awkward when you heard pow-wow songs. You wanted to run away and hide because you were ashamed of who you were. You hated being an Indian. The old ways were not for you anymore; they were for the ones who still lived on the reserve and understood the languages of long ago. You were now a little brown white man who didn't know much about anything and you felt shy whenever you went home because everyone was talking about how much you had changed!

You moved to the cities to forget and the streets became your home; jails became your refuge from the cold winter months, and you watched helplessly as your children were taken from you because you couldn't raise them properly. You drank to forget. You drank to celebrate your release from jail and you drank to feel good. You drank because you had too many problems and you had too many problems because you drank too much. You were labelled a deviant to society. Judges shook their heads as they reviewed your file and gave you another thirty days, and the only ones who understood you were the other Indian residential school outcasts!

Table of Contents

Introduction 1

My Early Childhood – The Happy Years 3

Chapter 1 – Please Don't Leave Us Here 14

Chapter 2 – The Unbearable Loneliness 31

Chapter 3 – We Just Want to Go Home 91

Chapter 4 – The Lonely Fall Season 120

Chapter 5 – Christmas Holidays at Home 161

Chapter 6 – A Cruel Winter 178

Chapter 7 – Home for Easter 216

Chapter 8 – Back to That Horrible Place 230

Chapter 9 – Reminiscing About Home 265

Chapter 10 – Endless Days of Summer 293

Introduction

Marieval was an Indian residential school I attended for six years. I was sentenced to this prison for being an Indian. The conditions were so harsh and traumatic for me as a child, a little boy in grade-one, that they can never be forgotten. The following is my story and first-hand account of the time spent at this residential school.

Marieval was run by Catholic priests and nuns who controlled the students with a strict code of conduct. Parents were discouraged from visiting their children during the school year to separate them from their families.

At school, life was unbearable as I described it after returning from my summer holidays.

My home was more than a hundred miles away. I would not hear Grandpa's stories for a very long time. I was stuck at this residential school where it was wrong to be an Indian.

Today, my name would be replaced by a number, and I would have to come running when they called it. Any mention of my culture was forbidden, so I would have to be careful not to break this rule. After all, my pagan ways were considered to be the work of the devil, and I was told to pray for my ancestors because they were probably burning in hell.

Another thing I learned was to watch out for bullies because of the lateral violence here. Some of the older boys liked to pick on the younger ones and make them cry. This violence stemmed from the nuns, priests, and staff who hit the students with rulers, keys, and straps to vent their anger.

I lived in constant fear of making a mistake that was going to get me into trouble. In other words, I had to live a perfect life here. There was only one person who lived a perfect life on earth, and he was crucified. When he died on the cross, everyone was happy. I couldn't understand why Christians killed their god and celebrated it as a good thing.

I would long for the days of being at home where it wasn't wrong to be an Indian. I would miss my mom's home-cooked meals where I didn't have to wait for the sound of a bell to tell me I could start eating.

Back home, no one talked about going to hell where a devil waited for us with a pitchfork. Grandpa said we didn't commit sins. He called them "learning experiences," and each one was sacred because they taught us about life, and life is sacred. Grandpa was a wise man and there were many things the nuns and priests could learn from him. Oh, I forgot. We were heathens and our cultural ways were forbidden because they were the work of the devil.

My Early Childhood—The Happy Years

I was born in Arcola, Saskatchewan, on February 4th, 1954. My parents lived on the White Bear Indian Reserve near the town of Carlyle. My late father, Norman Kakakaway, was from the Cree Nation while my late mother, Hazel, was from the Assiniboine Nation.

Some of my fondest memories take me back to my maternal grandparents' place on the reserve. My late grandfather, Xavier James McArthur, was a very kindhearted man. When he attended an industrial school, there were too many students named James, so they called him Xavier James, which was shortened to X.J. McArthur.

He was approximately thirty years older than my grandmother, Maude McArthur. She agreed to marry him after his previous wife died. They travelled by horse and buggy to Arcola to get married and they lived happily ever after. But, that's not the end of this story.

Grandpa was a very hardworking man who built a log shack for Grandma, my mom, and her siblings. This was way before the Department of Indian Affairs built houses on our reserve, so there were many log shacks on White Bear.

My mom and aunties lived in that old log shack until they grew up and moved away.

As the years passed, my grandparents were given a newer house by the band, but it was only a two-bedroom house. The old log shack Grandpa built was in constant use by our extended family.

I have many fond memories of that old grey log shack. It kept us warm during the cold winter months. I could hear the winds howling outside, but at the same time, I could hear the crackle of the fire in the heater and the woodstove. It felt cozy as we lay in bed all covered up with Grandma's patchwork quilts.

During the hot summer months, the mud kept the inside of the shack cooler than the outside temperatures. The house was protected by a front porch Grandpa built to prevent the wind from blowing into the house when someone opened the door on a windy day. The porch also served as a storage space for boots, tools, and the firewood needed for warming the house and cooking our food.

My dad was a hardworking man who always managed to put food on our table. He loved to hunt and often brought home deer, moose, or elk he shot in the park. Other times, he snared rabbits and prairie chickens during the winter. His love for hunting also included ducks and geese, which were plentiful in the sloughs near our place. Of course, at times he brought home groceries from town; we never went hungry.

Dad would also find work on nearby farms as a hired hand. During harvest, he would be up before sunrise and in the fields until well after dark. He worked long hours stoking and hauling the sheaves to the threshing machine.

As I grew older, I saw him driving tractors and pulling cultivators and harrows. There were times when I saw him picking heavy rocks by hand. Mom and I would often take him lunch when he worked in the fields because he didn't have time to come home and eat.

It was fun walking through the field. Although I was very young, I remember the time a bull chased us. We barely made it through the barbed wire fence before the bull came charging up to us. The scar remains from where my ankle was cut on the fence.

We moved around a lot working for different farmers. Because we were poor, Dad often bought used cars for work or transportation. When we weren't in the car, we lived in a large white canvas tent with a stovepipe sticking out of the top. Dad put a stove in the tent so Mom could use it for cooking and to keep the tent warm at night.

When Dad couldn't find work, he cut pickets to sell to local farmers for ten cents a picket. It was hard work, but the local farmers and ranchers always needed pickets for fencing in their cattle and livestock.

In the winter, we lived off the land and supplemented our diet with food rations from the Indian agency or groceries from Carlyle. As children, we did our share by setting rabbit snares. Prairie chickens and grouse would also get caught in our snares because they ran along the same rabbit trails to get through the bush.

The winds would howl outside as we sat around the supper table, but inside, the woodstove and airtight heater kept our house warm. We often shared a meal of rabbit stew, bannock or town bread, and some of Grandma's canned saskatoons, rhubarb, or raspberries.

We played a little game with the rabbit head at the end of the meal. Someone would ask the rabbit a question then throw the head into the air so it would land on the table. For example, "Who is going to be rich when they grow up?" The rabbit head would point to one of us and we would all have a good laugh. That lucky person would then get a chance to ask the rabbit the next question before throwing the head into the air. It was a fun game, but you could only ask the rabbit three questions, much like the genie in the lamp who only grants three wishes.

My grandparents worked hard in the summer planting and growing a garden. When the wild berries were ripe, Mom and Grandma would take us to the bush so they could pick them. We would spend hours on the land, the children playing in the shade and the adults filling their pails with ripe berries. Some of their favourite berries were saskatoons, raspberries, gooseberries, and chokecherries. Grandma canned a lot of the berries she picked and made jam from the rest. Sometimes we would sell berries to the cottagers at Carlyle Lake for spending money. Those were fun times because it meant we would be getting ice cream and pop from Hotel Beach or the store at Sandy Beach. Mom would let us go into the water for a good swim with the other kids, who were swimming in the lake to escape the hot weather.

Quite a few people swam there, but there were also the ones from the reserve who played on a raft anchored near the shore. For the better swimmers, there was a wooden diving tower a little farther from shore. Watching people dive from the top platform was an enjoyable way to pass the time. As far back as I can remember, our summer days were filled with adventure and excitement.

One afternoon, my older brother, Norman, and my younger brother, Oranges, convinced me to go with them to a nearby slough and catch little ducklings in the water. We managed to catch three and kept them as our pets. We didn't know they needed to be in the water with their mother. So, by the end of the day, all three of them died on us. From that experience, we learned not to bother the ducklings anymore. However, we did catch frogs, butterflies, and dragonflies near that slough.

Another time, Oranges went to sleep without emptying his pockets. Mom was going to wash his jeans, so she checked his pockets and screamed when she felt something cold and slimy in one of them. She handed his jeans to Dad and asked him to empty the pockets. Dad laughed when he pulled out a bullfrog.

We explored every trail and knew where all the birds' nests and beehives were located for miles around. We climbed trees and made slingshots for hunting birds and squirrels. Although we never killed anything with our slingshots, they were nice to have because nearly every young boy on the reserve had one. We saw them in the back pockets of our friends and thought that was cool.

Norman was good at making slingshots. He would take me to the bush and ask me to help him. First, he would find an ash tree and cut a branch with a good fork in it. Then he would peel the bark off the stick and make sure the fork had the right curvature. He used an old tire tube Dad had thrown away and cut some long narrow strips from it. Next, he had me stretch the rubber strips as tight as I could while he tied them to the slingshot handle. So, there I was pulling rubber strips with all my strength while he took his sweet old time tying the rubber to the handle. Sometimes he would stop what he was doing and scratch his forehead or shoo a fly away. I would tell him to hurry because my little arms were beginning to shake from exertion.

I enjoyed sleeping in the great outdoors and have fond memories of living in a large white canvas tent. Mom placed some mattresses on the ground and that became our bed.

During the night, we often heard animals approaching our tent. We would dive under our blankets and lay there quietly until they left. Then we whispered, "I wonder what that was? Maybe it was a Goo-can." I heard stories of ghosts and it was scary thinking about them. Although we didn't know it at the time, it was probably just some curious animals coming to investigate why the tent was in their bush.

During the summer, we climbed trees and explored the surrounding areas where Dad pitched our tent. He often cut pickets for days. When he got paid for them, we would drive into Carlyle for some gas, groceries, and treats.

Mom made bologna sandwiches and fed us in the car because it was too expensive to eat inside the Carlyle Cafe. Dad bought us delicious and healthy treats to go along with our sandwiches.

We waited patiently in the car for him to get back with a variety of different flavours of pop to choose from. Sometimes he had orange, root beer, grape, cream soda, or lemon-lime. The different colours made the choice a difficult one. This was before the price of pop became inflated and Dad probably paid less than a dollar for six drinks.

My parents and maternal grandparents

From left to right are my dad, Norman, my mom, Hazel, who is holding my younger sister, Bernadine. My brother, Oranges is sticking his head out the window. Grandpa X.J. and Grandma Maude are standing on the right. This picture was taken by my late aunt, Mabel McArthur.

Those were happy times and my life was carefree. Although our parents drank occasionally, I never knew our grandparents to drink, so I felt safe around them. Our parents and grandparents all attended residential schools. My siblings and I are third-generation survivors.

My grandparents never forgot about life in the bush and knew how to live off the land. They knew how to work hard. Grandpa X.J. once owned a herd of cattle and some heavy draft horses for pulling wagons, sleighs, and haying implements.

A few times Grandma asked me to tag along with her and take lunch to Grandpa when he was cutting hay in the sloughs near our place. He would stop his team of horses when he saw us coming.

I marvelled at him sitting up there on his steel seat with the reins in his hand.

He would smile at me and ask, "What did you bring me for lunch?"

Although I was scared of his horses, I tried not to show it. I think he knew I was afraid. However, he just smiled and reached for his lunch. Those were the early years when machinery was still pulled by draft horses.

The Indian agent, Mr. Anderson, lived in a large three-story mansion on the east end of the reserve. He was an extension of Indian Affairs and controlled the activities on White Bear. He ensured school-aged children were in school, during the school year. But he also distributed food bi-weekly to all the band members.

Grandma called them "ration days." During those times, we went down east to the red barns to receive our rations: salted bacon, canned goods, rolled oats, flour, tea, baking powder, sugar, salt, and potatoes. At certain times of the year, he also gave out vegetables.

On one occasion, Mr. Anderson, who lived across the road from the red barns, came over and invited Mom and Dad to come and visit him. Mom didn't tell us everything they talked about, but she did say Norman and I were going to be starting school at Marieval and Mr. Anderson was going to make all the arrangements.

Dad told us he attended Marieval until he was sixteen years old. He referred to it as Crooked Lake, which is one of the lakes near the school in the Qu'Appelle valley.

In the residential school era, the government forced parents to send their children to boarding schools where they could be assimilated into the dominant society. If a family refused to send their children to these residential schools, the R.C.M.P. would be notified. The parents could be arrested and sent to jail for non-compliance with the orders from the Indian Agent.

Mr. Anderson kept a registry of all the families who lived on White Bear, so he knew the ones who had school-aged children. He sent them to Brandon, Gordon's, Lebret, or Marieval. By law, children had to be in school until they turned sixteen years old.

These schools were nothing short of brutal prisons where the Indian was beaten out of the child and traditional teachings were replaced by religion, classrooms, and a strict code of conduct.

Although I had a very happy childhood, I didn't know my life was about to change when I turned six years of age. Up until this time, I'd never heard of hell, but I was about to find out where it was located.

This is the beginning of my story at the Marieval Indian Residential School. The happy times I knew as a child would become memories, replaced by loneliness and fear. My parents would become strangers as I learned a different way of life. The great outdoors I knew as a child would be replaced by foreign teachings from the Bible. I was about to learn it was wrong to be an Indian.

Chapter 1 - Please Don't Leave Us Here

On Sunday morning, September 4th, 1960, I could feel the excitement in the air as I put on my new jeans and shirt Mom bought for this special occasion.

She frantically searched for my new shoes but couldn't find them anywhere. She asked Grandma if she had a small pair of shoes that would fit me. However, the only ones she could find were my cousin Shirley's old shoes, the kind made with an opening in the front for two toes to stick out.

"Mom, I don't want to wear Shirley's shoes."

"Don't be silly," she said. "You have to wear shoes, and no one will notice."

Today Norman and I were going to start school at Marieval Indian Residential School.

My parents and grandparents were up early for the long ride in their 1954 Ford sedan. Back in the day, the car seats were wide enough to easily fit four adults and two small boys in the vehicle. The three-hour drive was hot and dusty. We had the windows open to let in the cooler air as we drove down the gravel road from Broadview to Marieval.

As we pulled up to the school, Mom reached into a bread bag and pulled out a damp face cloth. She wiped the sweat and dust off our little faces.

I didn't pay much attention to her. I was too busy staring at this huge brick building that was going to be our new home. It was bigger than Mr. Anderson's house.

Dad pulled into the driveway and Norman started sniffling like he was crying. Dad said, "Well, we're here."

Our parents walked with us to the front of the building while our grandparents waited in the car. Later on, I would learn the front of this building was called the parlour.

As we went up the steps, two nuns and a priest came out of the building; they were expecting us. Mom and Dad didn't seem to be afraid of them, but I wasn't too sure if I should trust them or not because they looked scary. If our parents weren't around, I would be running for my life.

The priest wore a long black robe with a large cross tucked into his waistband and the nuns had similar black habits with white cloths on their foreheads.

They also had a white cloth over the front of their habit. They had large sets of beads hanging from their sides. The way they looked mesmerized and frightened me.

I had heard many supernatural stories back home, so I was wondering if these funny dressed people were ghosts.

Norman said, "Mom, I don't want to stay here. I want to go home with you guys."

The nuns and the priest were smiling as they shook hands with Mom and Dad. They introduced themselves as Sister Superior, Sister O'Deil, and the school Principal Reverend Royal Carriere. They also shook our hands, but for some reason, they wouldn't let go of them. They asked our names and I told them my middle name was Gary, and my first name was Robert.

Mom and Dad were slowly retreating down the steps.

One of the nuns asked, "Are you boys hungry?"

I said, "Yes, I am." I was too fascinated by their appearance to notice Mom and Dad were sneaking away. However, before I realized what was happening, Mom and Dad were halfway to the car when all hell broke loose.

Norman jerked his hand away from the nun who was holding him. He raced back to the car, but our parents were already closing the doors. He screamed, "Stop!" However, Dad started the car and quickly backed out of the approach.

I pulled my hand out of the strong grip of Sister Superior and raced after my brother.

Norman chased after the car. "Wait for us! Wait! Don't leave us here!"

Dad kept on driving and left us behind in a cloud of dust.

We raced after the car, scared and choking on the dust, while the nuns and Father Carriere chased after us, the black-and-white habits of the nuns were flying in the wind.

By now, I was crying while yelling for my brother to wait for me. When I think back to that time, I can only imagine how hard it must have been for Mom, Dad and our grandparents to leave us behind like that. They were all survivors of these residential schools and must have realized what we were going through.

Everyone in the car must have been crying with their hearts breaking because they had to leave the children they loved behind.

Eventually, my brother and I got tired, and the nuns and the priest caught up to us. They grabbed our hands and brought us back to the school with a stern warning not to do that again.

My brother wouldn't stop crying. "But I want to go home!" he kept telling them.

I held his hand and tried my very best not to cry.

Father Carriere escorted us to the boys' side of the building and introduced us to a boys' keepers, Mr. Gilbert.

He told us we could stay inside or go out to the playground. He mentioned where the school boundaries were. "You're not allowed to go outside of the schoolyard."

We stayed in the playroom and sat on the wooden benches that were attached to the concrete walls while some of the other boys stared at us.

Then to our amazement, our cousin, Ernest, came out of the washroom with a big grin on his face and asked, "When did you guys get here?"

I can't remember what we said because I was so glad to see him. Ernest was the same age as Norman, but he started school here at Marieval a year ago.

We grew up with Ernest, so we were so happy to see him.

"Where's your sister Shirley?"

"She's on the girls' side, but it's off-limits to us."

He paused for a moment, shuffling his feet around. "Each of you is going to be given a number, and instead of being called by your name, you'll be called by that number."

I thought to myself, how will I remember my number when I don't know how to count yet?

Ernest brought us outside and showed us around the playground. Our playroom was in the basement and we had to climb a long set of cement steps to go outside.

Out on the playground, there was a steel set of swings, a couple of wooden sheds, monkey bars, wooden seesaws, two ball diamonds, a football field complete with uprights, and a new building called "The Block."

At four o'clock that afternoon, Mr. Gilbert blew his whistle on the playground and everyone returned to the playroom. When we were all assembled, we sat on the wooden benches.

I noticed the senior boys sat on the benches that were the closest to the dining room. The remainder of us sat around the room according to our ages.

Mr. Gilbert read the rules we were to follow. There were so many rules I didn't know if I could remember them all. Oh well, if I needed to know something, I could always ask Ernest. Some of the basic rules included: no leaving the schoolyard, the girls' side was off-limits, no fighting or rough play, and no swearing or cursing.

We were to sit and line up according to our numbers when they were assigned. We had to be silent when we heard a bell ring during meals and no wasting food. No going upstairs unless accompanied by a supervisor, the dining room was off-limits, and no running away or we would be strapped or severely disciplined. We were to address the two supervisors, as "Sir." And we were not to speak any language other than English while we were at school.

We were then assigned numbers starting with the senior boys. By the time Mr. Gilbert reached me, the numbers were getting larger. My number was sixty-seven.

I was told to remember my number and to come when they called it. I can't remember what Norman's number was because he was sitting beside Ernest when Mr. Gilbert was giving out the numbers.

After our supervisors finished talking, Mr. Dennis went through a door to the dining room and came back with a large metal bowl filled with apples. He started on the senior boy's side of the playroom and instructed everyone to take only one apple.

I was happy when he got to where I was sitting because, in all of the excitement, I had forgotten how hungry I was feeling. That apple sure tasted good.

When we finished eating our lunch, Mr. Dennis unlocked a wooden cabinet and opened the doors to reveal a large television set.

We didn't have electricity back home, so when he turned on the television, I was amazed to see people talking inside this strange box. When no one was looking, I checked behind the box to see how people got in there or if I would be able to see the back of them as they spoke. This was simply amazing! The picture was in black and white, and the reception came through a pair of rabbit ears on top of the set. There was no such thing as cable back then, so Mr. Dennis adjusted the antenna to bring the reception in clearer.

While the senior boys played outside, the newcomers like Norman and me were told to line up to see the seamstresses on the third floor. Two of them were waiting for us.

The one who met with me was a jolly old lady who liked to laugh. She wore a large-flowered dress and sat behind a sewing machine with a tape measure around her neck. Her name was Ms. Gregory, and it was nice to see an Indian lady working here. She asked what my number was, but she asked it amusingly. She said, "What's your number, cucumber?" It made me relax and I was happy to meet her. She also asked, "Where are you from?"

When I told her who my dad was and where I was from, she smiled. I could tell she knew him. I was lonesome and this nice lady brought a ray of sunshine into my heart.

As she talked, she sewed number sixty-seven into the back of my shirts and my other clothes. This number would become my new name.

When she was done, she sent me down to the playroom.

There, my brother and I sat quietly watching television until Mr. Dennis turned it off.

He went outside and blew his whistle to call in the boys who were playing outside.

When everyone was inside, he told us to go to the washroom and get ready for supper. He also informed us if we used the toilet, we could use only three squares of toilet paper. To make matters worse, the washroom did not have enough sinks, so the smaller boys stood back and let the bigger boys wash up first.

After everyone was done in the washroom, we sat in the playroom waiting for further instructions.

At the sound of a bell ringing, we were told to line up in four rows according to our numbers.

We entered the dining area in a single file. There were rows and rows of tables with benches on both sides of each table. The boys sat on one side of the dining room while the girls sat on the other.

The supervisors had their dining room located on the boys' side. I could see a large table with chairs all around it and some of the senior girls served them food from the kitchen. For added privacy, they kept their door closed.

Before we could eat, Sister Superior rang a bell and called for silence. She laid down the law in a very stern voice and told us we were to eat everything on our plates. None of the food was going to be wasted.

After she finished speaking, she began to pray.

Some of the older students prayed along with her. Of course, I didn't know what to say because I had never heard prayers before.

Oh well, I was hungry and happy when it was time to eat. There were about twelve of us sitting at our table.

A server brought over two pitchers filled with milk. We filled our cups and passed the milk pitchers around. We were given instructions to hold the pitchers above our heads when they were empty, and someone would fill them again.

I sat beside my brother and Ernest while some of his friends sat across the table from us. I met John, who would later become one of our protectors if someone bullied us.

He said, "If anyone tries to pick on you let me know."

I smiled after he said that because it made me feel safe.

When we were almost done eating, Sister Superior rang her bell and told us to finish eating the rest of our food in silence. By then I had already cleaned my plate, but one of the small boys didn't like his vegetables, so a nun went up to him and yelled at him to finish eating his food.

I pitied him as he sat there crying and forcing himself to eat. I wanted to go and eat his vegetables for him, but I knew if I left my seat, I would be in trouble, so I mentally cheered him on.

After several minutes, he swallowed the last of his food. Good for you, I thought to myself.

Sister Superior then told us how fortunate we were to have food when some of the children in Africa were starving.

I wondered why we couldn't save some of our food for the starving children she was talking about. Back home, we shared our food with all the people who came to visit us.

After everyone was done eating, a few senior girls collected our dishes and began washing them in a large sink.

I couldn't help but notice one of the girls had only one arm. I wondered what happened and how she could wash dishes with only one arm. That was many years ago and I never did learn who she was or what happened to her arm.

Before we left the dining room, we prayed and gave thanks for the food that was provided by the Lord, whoever he was. He sounded like a good guy to me.

After praying, we were dismissed to the playroom and some of the boys went outside for a ball game. This was the first time we ever watched a ball game, so Ernest explained the rules of the game to us. It was a hardball game, and the ball they used was made of stitched leather.

Mr. Gilbert was the umpire. He wore a mask and a chest protector in case he got hit by one of the pitches.

After I began to understand the rules, I started to loosen up a bit. In my mind, I began rooting for one of the teams.

Several houses were located beyond the schoolyard. I was curious about the houses, so I asked Ernest who lived there

He pointed to each house and told me who lived in them. One of the houses belonged to Mr. Lang, the principal of the higher grades. He had a nice blue and white house with a big front picture window.

I could see some bikes parked in front of the steps, so I assumed he had children.

Ernest told me he had three children—Bobby, Michael, and Ann—who attended our classes during the day. Ann would be in grade-one with us.

I watched two boys come out of the house, get on their bikes, and ride in the direction of the store. I didn't know how to ride a bike yet, so I was fascinated by how fast they could go. It wasn't long before the two boys rounded a corner and disappeared out of sight.

The afternoon passed so slowly. After the ball game was over, I sat on a swing for a while and watched a boy twirling around on one of the swings. I thought I would give it a try. I twisted the chains around as tight as I could then sat back and let them untangle. It was fun for a while but then I felt nauseous.

I left the swings and walked over to the monkey bars where some boys were hanging upside down. I climbed up the bars, but when I got to the top, I chickened out. That was too scary for me. I felt much safer on the ground.

As I walked around the schoolyard, I noticed a new brown building just a few yards south of the main brick building. It still had mounds of dirt piled around it. I pointed to the new building and asked, "Hey Ernest, what's in that brown building over there?"

"Oh, everyone just calls it 'The Block.' It's a new six-classroom building. It has a gym, home economics, and industrial/manual arts rooms. Both residents and day scholars will be attending classes there." He went on to say, "That is where classes for grades three to eight will be held."

I looked at the new building as he spoke. "That sounds good, but where are the grade-one and two classrooms?"

"The grade-one classroom is on the main floor above the boys' playroom, and the grade-two classroom is down the hall from it."

Since this was his second year at Marieval, I thought he was in grade-two, but he said he failed last year, so he was going to be in the same class as us. "The grade-one classroom was in the church basement last year. We had to walk there for class every day."

As he spoke, I tried to imagine what it looked like inside "The Block" and I found myself wishing I was in grade-three. I walked around the schoolyard some more. Steep hills near the school, captured my attention because they were unlike the hills we had back home. From deep inside came a desire to climb the trails leading to the top of those hills.

Ernest told me, "Sometimes we go for walks and climb those hills." Part of me cheered when he said that, but the other part was frightened at the thought of climbing them. What if I fell and got hurt? They looked very steep. Then I noticed some bushes behind one of the ball diamonds. The burble of water running from a creek came from somewhere below that little ravine. The creek was out of bounds.

I walked along the fence and wondered if anyone would chase after me if I decided to run away. I gradually made my way back to the swings and sat there feeling the loneliness of the day. I wondered what Mom and Dad were doing and if I would ever see them again. I could feel tears welling up in my eyes, so I put my head down and cried. I was still sniffling when someone put a hand on my shoulder. When I looked up, it was Norman.

"Don't cry. Mom and Dad will come and get us soon." In my heart, I wished that was true, but something was telling me we were going to be here for a very long time.

I looked around to make sure no one was listening, then I told Norman "I want to go home. I want to see Mom and Dad again. Do you think they'll let us go home if we ask them?"

He looked at me and said, "I don't think so."

When it was dusk, I heard a whistle blow. Then Ernest said, "It's time to go inside."

So, we returned to the playroom where the television was on. Norman and I joined some junior boys who were sitting on the floor in front of the television while the senior boys sat on metal and wooden chairs behind us.

I was still amazed at the way the television worked.

Chubby Checker doing "The Twist" had my full attention. The audience cheered and clapped as this black man sang and danced.

As the day turned into evening, a supervisor came into the playroom with a grey blanket containing shorts of various sizes and colours. "Okay, boys. It's time to take a shower."

I picked out a small pair of green shorts to wear.

Some of the senior boys who knew the routine well quickly jumped into the shower and claimed a faucet for themselves.

I stepped into the shower room. Before I knew what was happening, someone grabbed me and placed my face under the running water. I was fighting for my breath when I noticed it was a supervisor.

He grabbed a bar of soap and started to lather me with it. He washed me all over with that bar of soap.

I didn't like some of the places he washed me. When I struggled to get away, he stuck my face under the water. I thought I was going to drown from all the water I swallowed. I must have been in there for an eternity.

His musty smell and the body odour coming from his hairy armpits choked me. Thick and coarse chest hair abraded my bare skin as he pulled me up against him time and time again.

I knew this wasn't right because my dad never did this to me. It made me feel even dirtier than before I had the shower.

As soon as he reached for another boy to scrub with that bar of soap, I scampered away. I had to deal with showers that made me feel traumatized and violated every week. Who could I tell? Who would believe me? Probably just my parents and grandparents, but they were not around.

After we finished taking our shower, it was bedtime for the junior boys.

Mr. Gilbert called out the numbers for the ones who had to go to bed. When he called my number, I lined up with the rest of the junior boys.

I was afraid of being alone in this old brick building with creepily dressed people, so I was glad it was bedtime for Norman and Ernest too.

We went up several flights of stairs to get to a dorm where we were given a pair of pyjamas from one of the closets, then assigned beds.

Norman was going to be sleeping in the bed next to me. We were both on bottom bunks with other boys on the top.

After we put on our pyjamas, we were handed a toothbrush and told to line up for toothpaste. It wasn't toothpaste but a white powder kept inside a large silver can.

Mr. Gilbert put a scoop of it in my hand and said, "Go stand by the big sink over there and brush your teeth." This would become one of our regular rituals before going to bed.

We were also shown where the washroom was located. It had two toilet stalls and three urinals in it. This washroom was much smaller than the one located downstairs.

Mr. Gilbert said, "I'm going to turn the lights out after nine o'clock when the senior boys come to bed. For tonight everyone will be sleeping in this senior boys' dorm."

Chapter 2 - The Unbearable Loneliness

I felt so lonely that night and cried when the lights went out. As I lay in the dark, I could hear Norman crying too, so I reached over to him and held his hand. I whispered to him, "Everything is going to be alright. Mom and Dad will come and get us soon." I fell asleep listening to other boys crying in the dorm.

During the night, I woke to the sound of footsteps creeping up the stairs. I stuck my head under a woollen blanket, wondering if this was a boogeyman coming. I peeked and watched a man walk to a steel case on the wall.

He left a key dangling out of it. Then he shone his flashlight ahead so he could see where he was going.

I learned later he was the night watchman.

The supervisor had his bedroom on that floor. Shortly after the lights were turned out, he made several rounds to make sure everyone was asleep.

I wanted to ask him when we were going home, but I didn't want to get into trouble because I was supposed to be sleeping. This was a very strange and creepy place. I didn't want to be here and started to entertain thoughts of running away. However, I was only a small boy and had no idea how far away my home was or how to get there. The car ride here had taken about three hours. I would never be able to walk that far, so I was stuck at this school feeling abandoned, homesick, and traumatized. What was happening to us? Why did we have to be here? When was this nightmare going to end? I hated this place!

Mom and Dad never talked about this school, so I was confused and in shock.

That night I dreamt I was back home, playing down by the slough with my two brothers. We were swimming in the warm water and a mother duck swam by with her little ducklings following her. We played around in that slough until we heard Mom calling us to come and eat.

Grandma and Grandpa were in my dream too. It sure was nice listening to Grandpa telling his stories again.

My heart sank when I woke up and looked around me. It had only been a dream. I had to use the washroom, but I lay there for a long time wondering if it was going to be okay if I got out of bed.

After I couldn't wait any longer, I decided to go for it. I concentrated on a red light above the washroom and focused on it so I wouldn't bump into anyone's bed.

After I used the washroom, I tiptoed back to my bed. Beneath my blanket, I found myself wishing I could return to that dream where I was back home, but it never happened.

In the morning, I woke up confused and scared, looking around the room. Where was I? How did I get here? Then it all came flooding back to me. I was at Marieval Indian Residential School.

My brother sat up in the bunk next to me while Mr. Gilbert came out of his bedroom and told us to get up.

He showed us how to make our beds and how our pyjamas were to be neatly folded and placed underneath our pillows. He said, "I want all the pillow openings to be facing towards the big sink."

After Mr. Gilbert finished speaking, I raced to the washroom only to find there was a line up to use the urinals.

While standing in line waiting for my turn, a few senior boys behind me were telling me, "Hurry up, you're not the only one who has to use the washroom."

I went back to my bed after I finished in the washroom and changed into my clothes. I made my bed and neatly folded my pyjamas before placing them under my pillow.

Then I joined a line of boys who were waiting to get their powdered toothpaste. As I brushed my teeth in front of a crowded sink, I could see some boys taking their bedding downstairs.

Ernest whispered, "Some boys wet their beds regularly, so they're called 'firemen' by the other boys and they sleep close to the washroom at night."

As they carried their sheets downstairs to the laundry room, the boys who wet their beds were mercilessly teased by some of the senior boys.

I could see quite a few, maybe as many as five or six, who took their sheets downstairs.

We had to wait for them to return to the dorm and allow them time to make their beds.

In the meantime, some of the senior boys did their chores. One of them, Silly Butcher, cleaned the floor with a large white mop. He swept under all the beds and throughout the dorm. When he finished mopping the floor, he went to the fire escape and pushed the door open.

I was curious, so I went to the door and watched him as he shook out his mop. I was going to take a step out the door but looked down and froze. This was very high up and that was a long way down. I was afraid of heights, so I hoped mopping the floor would never be my job. I turned and walked away from the fire escape, dreading the thought of ever having to use it.

After everyone finished making their beds and doing their chores, we lined up and headed to our playroom.

We were instructed to sit on the benches according to our numbers and wait for the dining bell to ring so we could go for breakfast.

After the bell rang, we lined up and marched single file into the dining room. I was lucky enough to sit at the same table with Norman and Ernest.

Before we could eat, Sister Superior rang a bell and called for silence. She greeted us and told us to pray with her for the food we were about to receive. The warm porridge was lumpy and the toast dry. It couldn't compare to Grandma's porridge and the thick fried bacon she often cooked for breakfast.

When nearly everyone had finished eating their breakfast, Sister Superior rang her bell. "No more talking! Finish eating your meal in silence!"

Before we left the dining room, we prayed again. Why did we have to pray so much?

After breakfast, still more students arrived. A supervisor escorted them upstairs to see the seamstresses.

Some of the smaller ones looked like they wanted to cry and I could relate to them.

While they were gone, a few junior boys played floor hockey on their hands and knees, using a small rubber ball for a puck. When they noticed me and Norman sitting on the benches, they asked, "Hey, do you guys want to join us?"

I got to play the goal for our side, but it was easy to score on me as I had never played this game before.

When we started to lose, a boy named Stanford said, "You play forward and I'll be the goalie."

I wasn't much of a good player as a forward, so Stanford was getting upset with me.

Norman told him to leave me alone or he was going to bust him up. After that, Norman's nickname became "Boxer." Naturally, I was known as "Little Boxer."

Nearly everyone there had a nickname and I pitied my cousin Ernest because his nickname was "Pig-head." I never asked him how he got that name. I just called him Ernest because he was like a brother to me.

Our game was interrupted when Mr. Dennis came into the playroom. "I want you boys to check the bulletin board because I've posted numbers with chores to be completed throughout the day." As it turned out, my number wasn't on the list so there was no need to worry.

The other supervisor, Mr. Gilbert, told us we wouldn't be starting classes until tomorrow. "Go outside now so the senior boys can sweep and wash the floors."

More boys arrived at the school throughout the morning, adding to the number of boys who were already at school.

Outside, a few of them were playing a game of "scrub." They played at the senior boys' ball diamond, which was the better one of the two diamonds. Even though I didn't know the rules of the game, it was fun to watch.

Norman and I sat on a bench while Ernest picked up a glove and joined the game.

He said, "You guys want to grab a glove and join us?"

Norman replied, "No, thanks. We would rather watch."

Some of the senior boys were quite good at batting and catching the ball.

We watched the game for a couple of hours before we heard a whistle blow. It was time to get ready for lunch.

Everyone headed down the cement steps and into the washroom. There was a row of sinks and a mirror above each sink for us to wash our hands. There were four urinals, three toilets, and a shower room with faucets attached to the walls.

The senior boys claimed all the sinks for themselves while the junior boys waited in line for their turn.

When the senior boys finished washing their hands and slicking back their hair with Brylcreem, they returned to the playroom. They sat on the benches along the walls, waiting for the junior boys to finish washing up for lunch.

The bell sounded, and a supervisor ordered us to line up in four rows with the junior boys in the last row.

We walked into the dining room in a single file and found our seats among the rows of tables set for lunch. A lot more students filled the dining room this afternoon.

After everyone was seated, Sister Superior rang a bell. "Silence!"

Some of the students were still whispering, but after she gave them a stern look, they quit talking.

"When I ring the bell, all conversation is to stop immediately." She welcomed the new students to the school and went over the rules of the dining room before saying grace. "It is important to pray before and after each meal."

Some of the boys didn't like the liver and onions on their plates, so they quietly traded their liver to someone who wanted an extra dessert.

I later learned this happened on the girls' side too.

Liver and onions brought back fond memories of times when Dad killed a moose or elk and none of the food was wasted. This dish was considered a delicacy back home.

A junior boy couldn't eat his liver. He sat there and cried while a stern nun stood over him.

"No one will leave this dining room until all the plates are empty," she said.

Naturally, everyone stared at him while he sat there gagging, crying, and trying to finish his liver. He ate tiny bites and eventually managed to eat the liver on his plate with the help of a cup of milk.

We also had tapioca for dessert.

I never ate tapioca before, so I slowly picked at it when I overheard one of the boys say, "Fish eyes again." Now, for sure, I didn't like it.

Dad brought home fish during the spawning season, but he would always cut off the heads and we never ate the eyes.

I carefully picked at my dessert, but the tapioca didn't look like fish eyes to me; I knew what fish eyes looked like.

Although many of the students didn't care for this dessert, everyone had to finish what was put in front of them.

Near the end of our meal, Sister Superior rang her bell again and shouted for everyone to finish eating in silence.

Before we left the dining room, I listened as some of the senior boys and girls joined Sister Superior in a prayer.

Later that day, I was sitting on a bench with Norman when one of the senior boys came up to us and introduced himself as Marvin Smoker.

He asked, "Where are you guys from? Who are your parents?"

"We're from White Bear," I said.

"Our parents are Hazel and Norman," my brother added.

He smiled and said, "I know your dad. He's my cousin." He kept smiling at us and called us "the Normans."

Then I remembered Dad talking about our late grandmother, Nancy Smoker from Kahkewistahaw, which was one of the neighbouring reserves near Marieval.

We were happy to meet Marvin. It was comforting to know we had another relative here at school.

At four o'clock that afternoon, we were assembled in the playroom when Mr. Dennis came out of the dining room with a box of bananas. He quietly distributed them around the room.

Mr. Gilbert said, "You are not allowed to speak 'Indian' here. Anyone caught speaking 'Indian' will be strapped for breaking the rules. He looked at the new students. "English is the only language that will be spoken here."

The white supervisors controlled everything. They told us when to go to bed when to get up when to do our chores when we could use the washroom, when we could eat, and when we could speak. They held all the authority here, and their rules were not to be questioned. Both supervisors were above all the boys, and when they spoke, we were to be silent and obedient. Strict discipline was constantly enforced here at Marieval.

At seven o'clock on Tuesday morning, the lights came on. It was time to get up, but I still felt tired. The sound of the supervisor's voice telling us to get up jolted me awake. I scrambled out of bed so I wouldn't get yelled at. There was a line up for the washroom, so I decided to change into my clothes, make my bed, and fold my pyjamas before I did anything else. The line up for toothpaste was longer than the one for the washroom, so I stood in line for the washroom.

The "firemen" removed their bedding and walked with their heads down to the stairs, where they waited for one of the senior boys to escort them to the laundry room.

Before long, they returned with clean sheets and pyjamas.

By the time I came out of the washroom, some of them had already made their beds.

When everyone was ready to go, we headed down the stairs to our playroom.

At breakfast, a server handed out slices of bologna to each table. We were told to take one slice and pass the rest on to the others sitting at our table.

I watched as some boys made a sandwich and ate it with their porridge. I decided to give it a try and it tasted pretty good, so I discovered a new way of eating porridge.

This morning, there was an orange included with our breakfast. I put mine into my pocket to eat later.

One of the nuns saw me and said, "Take that orange out of your pocket and eat it before you leave the dining room." She scolded me in front of everyone. "You are not allowed to take food out of the dining room! Do you realize how fortunate you are to have food while so many children in Biafra are starving?"

I didn't know where these children were, but I did notice everyone in the dining room staring at me for making a mistake that affected children in a far-off country. It was embarrassing and not a mistake I would make again.

That morning, I met a boy in the washroom who was slicking back his hair over a sink.

"Hi! What's your name?"

He said, "My name is Alvin, but everyone calls me Shickle. What's your name?"

"My name is Robert, but everyone calls me Gary."

He smiled and asked, "Where are you from? What grade are you in?"

"I'm from White Bear, and I'm going into grade-one."

He said he would be in my grade and lived along the valley in Cowessess. Like Ernest, he had failed his grade, so he would be repeating it this year. His older brothers attended Marieval, so his parents sent him here too.

When he finished combing his hair, he asked me if I would like some of his Brylcreem.

"Sure. I'll try some."

He showed me how to slick back my hair like some of the senior boys did. But, for some reason, it didn't turn out the way it was supposed to. At least it wasn't the same as Shickle's hair, but I liked the way it made my hair smell.

After we finished combing our hair we went back to the playroom. Shickle asked, "Have you ever played Chinese checkers before?"

"No, I've never played it."

So, he said he would show me how to play it.

We each gathered a set of coloured marbles and placed them in a triangle on the board.

"The first player to move all ten marbles across the board into the opposite triangle will be the winner."

I wasn't very good at this game, but it didn't take long for me to learn some better moves by watching him jump around the board and get all of his marbles into the triangle in front of me. I could tell he pitied me when I lost because he asked, "Would you like to try a game of checkers?"

For this game, we used a board with red and black squares on it.

He explained the rules of the game while he set up the board. It was different than Chinese checkers. In this game, we could capture one another's chips.

It didn't take Shickle long to capture all of mine.

We played another round, and although I played better in the second game, it was clear I was no match for him. We had barely finished our game when a supervisor called out, "Put away the games! It's time to get ready for class!"

The grade-one classroom was upstairs and my assigned desk was near the windows. Three other students were sitting in front of me.

Our teacher, Ms. Sedeski, was a young white lady in her early thirties. She was introduced by Sister O'Deil, who started our day by reciting the Lord's prayer.

Then she left and Ms. Sedeski. said "I am going to be your teacher and I would like everyone to call me Ms. Sedeski or teacher. Like many of you, this will be my first year at Marieval."

After introducing herself, she had us sing "O Canada" followed by "God Save the Queen."

Then she started taking attendance and asked us to raise our hands when we heard our names being called. As she read the names on the class list, I waited for my name, but she never called it. She read the name Walter Grant, but that wasn't my name, so I didn't raise my hand.

Then she asked me if my name was Walter Grant.

I said, "My name is Robert but everyone calls me Gary."

"Well, there's no Robert Gary on my list, so your name has to be Walter Grant."

"No, it isn't. You can ask my brother Norman."

He nodded in agreement with me, but that still didn't convince her.

"In my class, you will answer to the name of Walter."

From that day on, I became known by a different name because I couldn't convince my teacher my name was Robert Gary. Eventually, everyone called me Walter and that name stuck with me for years after I left Marieval.

Ms. Sedeski pointed out the big drawer under our desks. "Your spare books and papers are to be kept in there so everything on your desk will be neat and tidy. Remember where your desk is because you'll be sitting at the same desk every time you come to class."

I looked around the room and smiled at Norman and Ernest who were sitting farther back in the classroom. I noticed a few new students I hadn't seen before.

They must be the day scholars that rode the buses here this morning. Some of them smiled at me when I made eye contact with them while others ignored me, but that was okay because I didn't know them.

Above the blackboard was a picture of a white lady with a crown on her head and below that were letters of the alphabet. Ms. Sedeski used a yardstick to point to the letters as she pronounced them to us.

We repeated the alphabet a few times before she said, "I am going to teach you a song to help you remember them."

She started to sing "The Alphabet Song" and we slowly started to sing along with her: "A, B, C, D, E, F, G, H, I, J, K, L, M, N, O, P, Q, R, S, T, U, V, W, X, Y, and Z. Now I know my A, B, C's. Next time won't you sing with me."

That was a cool song, but how will I put all these letters together to write a letter to Mom and Dad? I wanted to write a letter home so they would be proud of me.

We had a short fifteen-minute break from 10:30 to 10:45 called recess. That barely gave us enough time to use the washroom or get a drink of water.

After recess, our teacher handed out some scribblers and big black pencils. She also gave us eight wax crayons, pink erasers, and a small bottle of glue.

Later on, we learned how to make glue, which looked more like paste. It was also the same colour as Cream of Wheat cereal.

I was tempted to taste it, but Ms. Sedeski warned us, "Do not eat the glue because it can give you a tummy ache."

After she finished speaking, I turned around to Geraldine, who was sitting behind me, and asked, "What is an eraser used for?"

She made a mark on her scribbler with her pencil and erased it. "It's used for correcting the mistakes you make."

So, I tried it on my scribbler and it worked.

Around eleven o'clock that morning, a new boy came into our class. One of the nuns introduced him as Richard. In time, he would become one of my best friends while I attended school at Marieval.

After helping Richard get settled in, our teacher gave us a reader called *"David and Ann."*

She had us turn to the first page and repeat after her. "Oh."

We turned the page to see a picture of a boy and his dog. He said, "Oh, oh."

On the third page, David said, "Oh, oh, oh, see Spot run."

On the fourth page, it showed a picture of David and Ann and their dog Spot.

On the fifth page, David told Ann "See Spot jump."

Ann said, "Oh, oh, oh."

On the next page, there was a picture of a cat named Puff. David and Ann had two pets that liked to run and jump.

Ms. Sedeski asked, "Can I have a volunteer to read the first few pages?" Silence filled the room.

Everyone was too shy to read from the book, so she asked "Maxine, are you willing to give it a try?"

In a muffled voice, Maxine began to read the sentences.

Our teacher had to help her in a few places, but she did quite well.

Maxine, a very small girl with her long black hair tied back in a ponytail, came from the Sakimay reserve and was smart for her age. She attended Marieval during the day and was known as a day scholar. She was lucky because she rode the bus home after school.

Ms. Sedeski let us read those first few pages in silence. That little book was interesting, so I tried to read ahead on my own but quickly ran into problems reading the words.

After a while, Ms. Sedeski told us to put our readers into our desks, and I wondered what we were going to do next.

After everyone had put their books away, she told us, "I want you to put your heads on your desks and close your eyes." From the front of the room, she told us to imagine it was raining. "You can hear the raindrops coming down ever so gently. Tap your feet on the floor to make the sound of raindrops coming down."

I tapped my shoes on the floor.

"It's starting to rain harder so tap your feet harder."

I tapped my feet a little harder.

As I did this, she said, "It's thundering and lightning. I want you to stomp your feet on the floor and clap your hands to make the sound of thunder and lightning."

I clapped my hands and stomped my feet on the floor until she told us to stop. This was a good game, and I hoped we would play it again.

At noon, the bell rang. Ms. Sedeski told us to line up and go back to our playrooms. She said, "Enjoy your lunch and I'll see you this afternoon."

Everyone said, "Good-bye teacher," and we headed down the stairs.

She was a nice lady. What new things will she be teaching us this afternoon?

As we returned to the playroom, I looked for Ernest.

When he came into the room, he asked "How is your little brother Oranges doing?" He still called him by the nickname he received when Grandpa caught him stealing his Mandarin oranges last winter. Another reason we called him that name was due to the sun bleaching his hair during the summer months and tinting it orange.

"He's probably getting lonely for us, but he's lucky to be at home with our parents."

I was going to ask him how he received his nickname, but I didn't want to offend him, so I didn't say anything about it. I knew Indians like to tease and give one another nicknames.

Someone called Richard "Buster" and although I was curious about that name, I never asked him about it either. I liked to talk to Richard because he was quiet like Norman, and it seemed like he needed a friend.

When we lined up to eat, I invited him to come and sit at our table in the dining room. "Richard, come and stand behind me so you can sit with us."

After Sister Superior said grace, we started to eat.

Ernest said, "Look on the girls' side. Some of them are waving at us." Sure enough, my cousin Shirley and some others were waving and smiling at us.

I felt shy because other girls from that side were staring at Shirley to see who she was waving at. The dining room was full as the day scholars had joined us for lunch.

A new boy was sitting at our table. Someone said his name was Morley and he lived across the creek not too far from the school but too far to walk home for lunch.

We had a special treat at lunch. Usually, the pitchers were filled with milk, but today they contained orange juice and were constantly being emptied because everyone wanted seconds and even thirds.

At home, we rarely had any juice to drink. There were times when Mom would bring home Freshie, which later became known as Kool-Aid. Other times, she would buy us pop, which she called soft drinks.

So today, we enjoyed having a sweet drink to go with our soup and sandwiches.

I was happy when lunch was over and we were allowed to go to the playground to play with our friends for a while.

Some of them asked, "How do you guys like it here?"

Norman said, "We don't like it. We want to go home."

One of them said, "I feel strange here too, and the nuns look scary and mean."

At one o'clock, the whistle blew and we knew it was time to go inside.

After everyone had congregated in our playroom, we went upstairs to our classroom where Ms. Sedeski greeted us with a smile. "This afternoon you are going to learn how to count. Does anyone know how to count?"

The only person who knew how was Maxine.

Another girl, Ann, later told us, "I know how to count, but I didn't want to say anything because I was afraid our teacher would ask me to count out loud."

Next, our teacher told us to take out our scribblers and write down numbers as she wrote them on the board. She wrote numbers from one to ten and asked us to repeat them several times while writing them in our scribblers.

She slowly went around the room, stopping at each student's desk and examining their work. When she came to my desk she said, "Very good, Walter, but try to keep your numbers between the lines."

It felt awkward writing down numbers with my big, fat black pencil. Then she asked me "Do you know how to use your eraser?" and I proudly said, "Yeah."

I didn't tell her Geraldine had shown me how to use it, but I'm sure she was listening to our conversation. Counting to ten and reciting our alphabets would become a part of our daily schedule until we knew how to count and recite our alphabets by heart.

When we finished writing down our numbers from one to ten on the first page of our book, Ms. Sedeski said "Now we are going to do something different."

She opened a cabinet and handed out plasticine strips and told us "We are going to make a sculpture of an animal that comes to mind."

My imagination wasn't very good, so I decided to make a dog like the one we had in our reader. I tried to remember how he looked, but I had trouble doing that so I pulled out my reader and kept the page open to where Spot was running.

By the time I finished my sculpture, it didn't even look anything like Spot. When I tried to make him stand up, one of his legs fell off. I looked around the room and watched some of my classmates making nice sculptures while others struggled as I did.

I went to the table where Ernest and Norman were working on their projects.

Ernest said, "I am making a buffalo like the one on TV."

My brother was sculpting a horse. He smiled and asked me, "How do you like my stallion?" His horse looked like it was the best artwork in class, and I felt proud of him.

I didn't tell him how I felt because he was always trying to compete with me at everything we did. In most cases, I accepted the challenge and tried to do things better than him, but all too often, I just couldn't measure up to him.

I showed him my plasticine figure of Spot and he laughed.

I walked over to Richard's desk to show him my dog.

He said, "Yeah, that looks like Puff in our reader."

I told him it was a dog, not a cat.

When he laughed, I returned to my desk.

Then our teacher asked me what I made. I showed her my work of art.

She said it looked like a nice cat and I had done a good job of sculpting it.

After everyone finished working on their little project, she asked us to bring our plasticine back to the cabinet where she put it away for future use.

We had our second recess from 2:30 to 2:45, which was a welcome break as I had to use the washroom and get a drink of water from one of the taps.

When we returned to class, Ms. Sedeski said we were going to play a game called, *"The Farmer in the Dell"*. She explained how the game was played and put on a record.

I was curious about her little record player, so I watched as she placed a record on there and it began to spin.

Next, she took the small arm and placed it on the record and you could hear a lady singing *"The Farmer in the Dell."*

Ms. Sedeski instructed us to hold hands and move around the circle in a clockwise direction until the music stopped.

Shickle was chosen to stand in the middle of the circle because he was the farmer.

Once again, the music started and we held hands while moving around the circle until the music stopped. Now the farmer, Shickle, had to choose a wife. One of the girls named Karen joined him in the centre.

When it came to Karen's turn to choose a child, she picked me. Once again, the music played and when it stopped it was my turn to choose a pet, and Norman gave me a stern look that clearly said, "Don't you dare pick me."

I knew that look and I would've been in trouble if I had chosen him to be my pet. So, I picked Richard to be the family pet.

Everyone in the class laughed and smiled at him for being the pet. It was fun while it lasted, and I wished we could have played it again.

We had just returned to our desks when there was a knock on our door.

Sister O'Deil. came in to talk to us.

Ms. Sedeski sat at the back of the room as Sister O'Deil told us about some stories from the Bible.

She explained the difference between venial sin and a mortal sin. "If you die with a mortal sin on your soul you are going to go to hell, but if you die with a small sin on your soul you will end up in purgatory."

She described what it was like in hell and how a devil named Lucifer would keep us in that place forever.

You burn in hell because there's a huge fire down there.

Then she shared a couple of stories about people who didn't believe in God.

Her first story was about a lady who scoffed at anyone who believed in Jesus Christ. Every time she met a Christian she would say, "There's no such place as heaven or hell" or "You're wasting your time going to church."

When she died, she was punished and sent to hell.

After that, she would often appear to people and ask them for water. She was so desperate she asked for just a small drop of water to be placed on her tongue.

Then Sister O'Deil said, "That's what is going to happen if you don't go to church."

Next, she spoke of a woman who ended up in an insane asylum in Weyburn. The lady did not believe in God. She mocked people for their beliefs.

One day, Jesus appeared to her and she went crazy.

Sister O'Deil said, "She's still in the asylum, and all she can say is, 'he has come, he has come.' She will spend the rest of her life in that asylum."

She finished by leading us in prayer before we were dismissed for the day.

The day scholars raced to catch their buses home. They were lucky; they would be seeing their parents and sleeping in their beds that night.

I was jealous and lonely at the same time, so I went outside to hang out with Norman.

He was the only brother I had here and it felt good being near him.

I knew he was feeling lonesome too because he was very quiet. There were tears in his eyes when I found him

We sat on the benches in the playroom waiting for a supervisor to pass around our lunch.

Soon we were receiving our afternoon snack; today it was oranges. I looked at my orange and asked Norman, "I wonder what our little brother Oranges is doing at home?"

He said, "He's probably being spoiled as usual."

We both laughed at the thought of our little brother Oranges playing at home.

After we finished eating our afternoon snack, Mr. Dennis informed us the junior boys would be sleeping in the small boys' dorm tonight. Bedtime would be at eight o'clock.

He called out the numbers for the ones who would be going to the junior boys' dorm.

As I expected, my number was on the list, but he called Norman's and Ernest's numbers too. He said, "I'll be taking you upstairs to show you where your dorm is and where you'll be sleeping tonight."

He had us line up according to our numbers and follow him to the dorm.

When we got there, a nun gave us clean pyjamas, toothbrushes, face cloths, and towels. Rows and rows of beds were in those two rooms. One room held about six bunk beds and it was near a washroom while the other room was connected by a corridor and it had about twenty single beds.

All of the single beds were placed in neat little rows, and they had white head and foot railings. They faced in the same direction and were neatly made up with white sheets and grey woollen blankets that were pulled tightly over the mattresses. It was like walking into a hospital ward.

As I surveyed the room, I wondered where I'd be sleeping for the night.

Ernest interrupted my thoughts. "I remember this dorm. This is where I slept last year." He pointed to one of the beds in the corner of the room. "Someone will give you a bed and that's where you'll sleep every night. Sometimes the junior boys who wet their beds, or become sick are placed in the room closest to the washroom, where the night supervisor has her bed and night table.".

"Who is our dorm supervisor?"

"Last year it was an elderly Indian lady everyone called Grandma Smoker, but sometimes, it's one of the nuns from the school."

This junior boys' dorm looked so much cozier than the larger dorm where the senior boys slept, but I didn't like the idea of going to bed while it was still daylight outside.

Back home, we didn't have to come inside until it was getting dark outside. Even then, we were allowed to stay up until it was too dark to see.

After everyone had neatly put away their belongings, we lined up and went back to the playroom.

When we got there, Mr. Dennis said, "It's too nice to stay inside so we're going for a walk to the dam but you are not allowed to go into the water."

Mr. Gilbert led the way along with a group of senior boys while Mr. Dennis brought up the rear with some of us junior boys. If we lagged too far behind, he would wait for us and tell us to hurry up. The dam wasn't very far from the school, and it was a warm afternoon for a walk.

Norman and I had never seen the dam before so Ernest described it and told us he went there on numerous occasions last year.

He said, "Sometimes people fish there, and it's near a beach where people often go swimming."

When we arrived at the dam, some of the boys were already walking across it.

I slowly stepped onto the walkway and looked down at the water below. One side was calm, but on the other side, water was gushing into the river.

I noticed a young man with a long pole that had a snare wire attached to the end of it. I asked him, "What kind of fish do you catch here?"

"There are different kinds of fish in the lake, but most of the time, I catch suckers."

He showed me one of the suckers he caught and it had a round mouth. It looked different than the fish Dad brought home. He liked fishing, especially during the spring when they were spawning.

I found myself getting lonesome and wanting to go home. Before I knew it, tears filled my eyes. I tried my best not to cry, but I missed Mom and Dad so much I couldn't help it.

I walked away from the group so I could have a good cry. Loneliness can be traumatizing for a little boy, but at Marieval, no one cared.

We walked around the dam for about an hour before Mr. Dennis blew his whistle and told us, "It's time to return to the playroom and wash up for supper."

As we walked, I marvelled at the valley, gazing at the hills and trees that grew along the ravines. We didn't have a valley like this back home, but we camped below Heart Hill one summer.

I don't think Heart Hill was as high or as steep as the ones here. I asked Norman "Can climb those hills?"

He said, "Of course, I can."

I wondered if he would ever get a chance to prove it.

Ernest pointed to a high hill near the school and said, "We went sliding on that hill last winter and it was fun."

I didn't think I would ever be able to slide down that hill because it looked too steep.

When we were getting close to the school, we walked by a house called the priests' rectory.

Ernest said, "This is where the priests live. Sometimes, visiting priests come to Marieval to offer sacraments, and this is where they stay."

I asked him, "How many people live in that house?"

He replied, "Right now, I think there are only two priests who stay there. The nuns have their dorm above our classroom." The rectory was conveniently built right next to the church so the priests didn't have to go far when they served Mass.

Mr. Dennis said, "Some girls are given chores to help make things easier for the priests. In the Roman Catholic religion, a priest is not allowed to marry. Therefore, he doesn't have a wife to help him with household chores."

As we walked by this building, the horrible memory of me and my brother chasing after our grandparents' car, screaming for them to stop for us, replayed in my mind.

Not wanting to think about that anymore, I distracted myself by wondering what was in the rectory because I never had a chance to see the inside of it. It was probably like other houses but with more crosses and holy pictures on the walls.

As we approached the girls' side of the school, I noticed some of them were still on the playground.

They had swings, seesaws, and a slide like we had, but in addition to that, they had a wooden glider bench.

Ernest said, "Sometimes the nuns sit on that bench and swing themselves back and forth as they talk."

That swing looked cool. I would like to ride it someday if I ever get a chance.

They also had a fire escape running along their side of the building as we had on our side.

Ernest explained, "When we have fire drills the girls have to come down those stairs." That looked high, very high, and I didn't look forward to fire drills.

Dad had shared stories of the time he went to Marieval and they didn't have stairs to use for a fire escape. They had to slide down a pole and land on hay at the bottom. Now that would be scary.

The girls' playroom was in the basement like ours and I wondered if Shirley was down there. If she was, what was she doing?

Off to our right, there was an old snow bus near the fence with the word *Bombardier* written on it. It could seat ten to twelve passengers.

Ernest said, "I never saw anyone using it last winter."

"Maybe if we're lucky and the snow is deep enough, we can go for a ride in it this winter," I said.

It looked like it would come in handy if the roads were blocked and we had to go somewhere. It reminded me of a modern version of a team of horses pulling a sleigh.

When we walked between the school and a big white building on the west side, Ernest said, "We're standing over a tunnel that connects the school to the boiler room and pump house. That white building is also where they keep our skates, hockey equipment, and winter clothes."

What would it be like to skate? I recalled watching our dad and our uncle skating on a slough back home, and it looked like it was a lot of fun.

When we returned to the playroom, Mr. Gilbert went to check on our supper while Mr. Dennis said, "I want everyone to wash up for supper."

Once again, the junior boys had to wait in line to get to the sinks while some senior boys took their time slicking back their hair and making sure they looked cool.

In the 1960s, it was common for boys to grease and slick back their hair with Brylcreem, a common brand of hair styling cream for men. The ones that could afford this styling cream put it in their hair.

I didn't worry about my hair because I wasn't interested in girls. I was more concerned about washing my hands and getting back to the playroom so we wouldn't get yelled at for being slow. I knew our supervisors could be short-tempered and mean. I didn't want that to happen if I could help it.

During supper, I had a chance to peek through an opening in the kitchen where I saw a nun dressed in white. Why did she have on a different coloured habit than Sister Superior and the other nuns? Maybe she was the cook and had to wear that colour when cooking our food.

She took a loaf of bread and put it into a machine then it came out in slices. She also picked up a pail of milk and poured it into pitchers for the servers to bring into the dining room. When she saw me watching her, she smiled at me.

I looked away as my face flushed. After I finished eating the food on my plate, I noticed a small corridor leading to another room. Where did that passage lead?

When the coast was clear, I peeked around the corner. Huge washing machines were along one wall and some big dryers on the opposite wall. A large sink was next to the washers and dryers. I had just discovered the laundry room.

At that moment, Sister Superior rang her bell, so I scurried back to my place before she noticed my empty seat.

After supper, Mr. Dennis informed all the newcomers they would be going to "The Block" next door to get their hair cut by Mr. Batza.

He said, "Line up and follow me."

Once we had formed a line, he took us to the east side of the building where we went downstairs to the basement. A gymnasium was on the right and another room on the left with a dentist's chair in it.

We kept going down a hallway and turned into a room on the right with table saws, lumber, and tools hanging on the walls. This was my introduction to the woodworking shop and the first time I met Mr. Batza.

He was a stern and grumpy-looking man that you wouldn't want to mess around with. He doubled as both a woodwork instructor and a barber. "Sit down on that bench and wait your turn," he said with a gruff voice.

He turned to Mr. Dennis and told him, "I'll send them back to their playroom when they're done here."

The supervisor left and we sat there in silence, waiting for our turn as we watched him clip the first boy's hair.

One by one, the junior boys left until there was only my brother and me left in the room.

I didn't know if I should go next or let Norman go first because one of us was going to be left alone with the barber.

That's when Mr. Batza spoke for the first time. "What are your names and where do you boys come from?"

Norman told him our names were Norman and Walter, and we came from White Bear.

When he finished cutting Norman's hair, Mr. Batza said, "You can have a seat and wait for your brother." Maybe he wasn't such a bad guy after all.

After getting my haircut, I went to the washroom to look in the mirror. I was in for a big surprise. I was shaved almost bald! My bat ears were sticking out and noticeable now. I kept rubbing my head, wishing my hair was longer so the senior boys wouldn't tease me about my ears. Maybe no one would notice.

I went to the playroom to watch television.

Norman looked funny too, but I didn't dare say anything to him otherwise he would box my bat ears.

We sat by Johnny in front of the TV.

"What are you watching?" I asked.

"It's called Wagon Train," he said.

Before long, I was interested in this Western show. I enjoyed shows about the Old West and could watch them for hours. I cheered for the good guys and laughed whenever an Indian got shot off his horse.

When the show was over, Mr. Dennis said "It's bedtime for the junior boys."

He escorted us upstairs and introduced us to our supervisor, who smiled when she saw us enter the dorm.

She was an elderly lady with very dark skin and grey hair. She sat near her nightstand and wore a long black dress with yellow and white flowers on it.

When the supervisor left, she said, "You can call me Grandma," so that's what we called her. She picked out the smallest boys including myself. "You are going to be sleeping in the same room with me so I can keep an eye on you in case you need anything."

I hoped Norman would be alright sleeping in the next room, but I felt better after Grandma Smoker checked on them, "They are putting on their pyjamas and getting ready for bed."

After we brushed our teeth, she made sure we used the washroom before kneeling and saying a short prayer beside our beds. She showed us how to place our hands together, close our eyes, and recite a prayer with her.

Before she turned out the lights, she asked me "Who are your parents?"

When I told her my dad's name, she smiled but didn't say anything. I was still lonesome for my parents and younger siblings. I didn't like this place and couldn't figure out why we had to be here.

I woke up the next morning and I was confused. How did I get here?

Then I realized I was in the small boys' dorm when I saw Grandma Smoker going into the next room. She turned the lights on and I heard her telling the boys it was time to get up. She told us to make our beds, and for some reason, she didn't go around checking them.

We washed our hands and face and brushed our teeth.

When everyone was ready, Grandma Smoker told us, "Line up by the exit door and wait for a supervisor to come for you. You have a nice day and I'll see you this evening."

Sure enough, at eight o'clock Mr. Gilbert came for us and we went down to our playroom.

On Wednesday morning as we waited for breakfast, Mr. Dennis informed us on Thursday a dentist would be visiting the school. All the boys in grade-one would be getting a chance to see him for a checkup. He read out the numbers for the boys who had dental appointments, and sure enough, my number was included. He also called Norman's number. Neither of us had ever seen a dentist before, so I was worried we were going to have some teeth pulled out. The rest of the boys would be seeing the dentist later.

I would have preferred to see him at a later date like next year or the year after that.

Mom had visited a dentist in Carlyle when she had a toothache. She was in a lot of pain when she came out of his office, so I wasn't looking forward to this appointment.

As we ate breakfast, I smiled at one of the senior boys I met earlier.

He smiled and kept eating. His name was Nick. He didn't say very much, so I thought I'd better leave him alone.

As I was eating my porridge, John smiled at me and said, "I see you met my older brother."

I looked at him and asked, "Is that your brother?"

When I looked at the two brothers, I noticed John was friendly and easy to approach whereas Nick was quiet and his personality was not so inviting. I guess you could say he was a good guy, but if you got on his bad side, he could bust you up.

The food we ate that morning wasn't very good and I missed my mom's fried deer meat and bannock. She was the best cook in the world, and the meals back home were always fun times.

We didn't have to finish eating our meals in silence and pray before and after each meal.

Gee, I wished I was at home. I felt lonely for Mom, and once again, I felt like crying. There were tears in my eyes, but I tried not to show it. I was in deep thought when I heard a big commotion coming from the dining room exit.

A fight had broken out, and a nun was trying to grab one of the senior boys. It looked like Uncle Marvin.

I saw a fist fly through the air and hit that nun on the nose.

Her head flew back and I could see blood running down her chin and staining the white part of her habit.

Almost immediately, the supervisors' door flew open and both of the male supervisors raced toward the fight. They grabbed Uncle Marvin and hustled him into the playroom while the girls' supervisor helped the injured nun out of the room. The whole dining room was abuzz and the students were asking each other, "Did you see what happened?"

Shortly after that, Sister Superior rang her bell and called for silence. "Remain calm and finish your meal in silence. There is no need for anyone to be afraid. You will all be dismissed in a few minutes."

When we were back in the playroom, I looked around for Uncle Marvin but I couldn't see him.

Mr. Dennis said, "Marvin is in the principal's office and he will likely be expelled from school. He may have broken that poor nun's nose when he punched her. There's a good chance the R.C.M.P. will be coming for him."

None of us said anything. We never did see Uncle Marvin in school after that. What would have made him lose his temper so badly that he punched one of the nuns?

Years later, I found out he had been tortured at Marieval. He had reached his breaking point. Although violence is not the answer to anyone's problems, he just couldn't take any more abuse. He was taught violence through strappings and other forms of physical abuse, so this was how he lashed out when he became angry.

As we sat there waiting for Mr. Gilbert to come down from upstairs, Mr. Dennis lectured us about violence and how it would not be tolerated here. "So, if anyone is thinking about doing the same thing, they had better think twice."

Shortly after that, Mr. Gilbert came back alone and said, "Okay, he's gone. He's out of here."

I guess it meant we wouldn't be seeing Uncle Marvin at school anymore. I was going to miss him.

When we were back in our classroom, Ms. Sedeski asked us, "Why do you look so sad?"

A student told her about the fight in the dining room.

"Oh, no! Is everyone okay? Anyone afraid?" she asked.

Although I felt a bit shaken up over the whole ordeal, I never said anything.

I was daydreaming as she spoke, thinking about a time when I saw Uncle Ernie hit Dad in the nose when he was drunk. I felt sorry for my dad and found myself wanting to be with him to make sure he was okay.

After we sang the national anthem, Ms. Sedeski said, "We are going to play Pin the Tail on the Donkey."

She lined us up in rows and told us to face the bulletin board where she had placed a large paper donkey. "The objective of this game is to close your eyes, take the donkey's tail, and try to pin it on the donkey."

Our row was the first to try it. When it was my turn, I couldn't help but peek a little.

She said, "Very good, Walter." But then she opened her little closet, pulled out a blindfold, and said, "Let's try this."

She put the blindfold on the next student behind me.

Geraldine looked comical as she reached for the board where the donkey was placed. The class laughed as she pinned the tail on the donkey's head.

I especially laughed at Richard because he missed the donkey altogether. One by one, the students tried their best to pin the tail on the donkey, but no one came as close as I did, so Ms. Sedeski gave me a prize for winning the game.

In hindsight, I'm sure she knew I peeked a little bit, but she didn't say anything.

After we finished playing that game, we pulled out our readers and our teacher carefully pronounced the words in our book about David and Ann.

She methodically went up and down the rows. Occasionally, she stopped at someone's desk and asked them to read a sentence to her.

I understood the sentences, but when she stopped at Norman's desk, I could hear him struggling with some of the words. I wanted to go and help him, but I knew if I did, Ms. Sedeski would tell me to go and sit down.

While all of this was going on, my cousin Burl was sticking his big fat pencil into his ear and scratching the inside of his ear with it.

Our teacher caught him doing that and sternly told him, "Put your pencil down and stop doing that. You can get an ear infection because your pencil contains lead."

Shortly after we were dismissed for recess, I saw a couple of junior boys swinging on the pipes in the playroom. It looked like fun, so I thought I would give it a try.

The other boys jumped down just before Mr. Gilbert came out of the washroom.

I was too late and he caught me dangling from the pipes.

He told me, "Get down from there! You're in trouble, Walter! I want you to come to the office after lunch."

The supervisor's office was located across from the washroom. I had never been to that office, so I was scared.

Ernest told me "You're probably going to have to kneel in the corner because that happened to some boys last year."

When we returned to class, I couldn't stop wondering what kind of punishment I was going to get for swinging on the pipes.

Back in class, our teacher was satisfied everyone could read the sentences in our book. "Tomorrow, you will be getting a new reader entitled *'Dick and Jane'*. It's an interesting book." She held up a copy for all of us to see. The book was a bit thicker than our first reader, and it probably had harder words, but I was happy we would be getting something new tomorrow.

Then she said, "Put all of your books into your desks. I am going to play some music for you." She pulled out a small record player along with a vinyl record and turned it on.

I watched the record as it started to spin.

We sat there and listened to the song *How Much Is That Doggie in the Window?*"

When it was over, she played it again and said, "Sing along with me."

If there's one thing I know about myself, it's that I'm not very good at art and I'm much worse at singing. First of all, I couldn't remember the words. Secondly, I was way out of tune. I was happy there were no dogs around because they would've been howling for sure while I was trying to sing.

Some of the girls caught on quickly and I could hear them singing along quite well.

Once we were dismissed for lunch, I slowly made my way to the supervisors' office. I quietly knocked on their door and hoped no one would answer.

Mr. Gilbert told me to come in and close the door.

I was scared when he asked, "Why were you climbing on the pipes?" I didn't want to rat out the others when he asked me who else was doing that. I told him, "It was just me and it looked like fun."

He said, "Well, I hope you find kneeling in the corner fun because that's what you're going to be doing right after lunch, and you're going to stay there until it's time to go back to class." He told me the next time he caught me doing that, I would be explaining everything to the principal.

I was happy to hear I wasn't going to get a strapping like so many of the other boys I heard about. Perhaps I got off lucky because kneeling in the corner couldn't be all that bad.

When he finished talking, he told me to go and wash up for lunch.

I raced to the washroom to wash my hands, and when I was done, I lined up for lunch.

The dining room door opened and I followed Norman. We sat next to Ernest, who looked like he was feeling sick.

He sneezed at the table and grabbed his nose as mucus came out; he caught it in his hand. He didn't have his handkerchief with him, so he asked around the table, "Does anyone have a hanky?" Poor Ernest sat there cupping his hands to his face and asking for help.

Then one of the nuns noticed him and said, "I'll be right back." She disappeared into the laundry room and came out with a red handkerchief. She told him, "Here. Use this one and keep it in your pocket in case you need it again."

After he blew his nose, I could feel a lump in my back pocket. I put my hand into my back pocket and pulled out a handkerchief. That was the one pocket I didn't check, so I told Ernest I was sorry for not helping him.

He said, "That's okay, I have one now."

We returned to our playroom when lunch was over.

Mr. Gilbert pointed to the corner of the room and said, "I want you to kneel in that corner. Don't look around or talk to anyone until it's time for class."

At first, it didn't seem so bad, but as the minutes went by, my knees began to hurt. I could hear some boys talking nearby, but I didn't want to ask them what time it was in case Mr. Gilbert was still in the room watching me. I listened for clues that would tell me what time it was. I knew we came back to the playroom around twelve-forty, and I had been kneeling here for about five minutes. Oh, good, it wouldn't be too much longer now. At least, that's what went through my mind, but have you ever knelt on a wooden bench for twenty minutes? It wasn't as easy as I thought, so I was relieved when it was time for class.

That afternoon, Ms. Sedeski showed us how to print our names. She told us to practice by putting our names on our scribblers and the papers she was going to hand out.

She gave us a page that contained different pictures and told us to write the correct name underneath each item. For example, if it was a picture of a ball, dog, cat, boy, girl, etcetera, we were to write the correct word on a blank line below the picture.

I had fun looking for the correct word and making sure I copied it down properly.

When I completed my work, I looked around the room.

There were a few others like Maxine, Ann, Geraldine, Ernest, and Shickle who were finished with their work.

Ms. Sedeski gave the class a few more minutes before she told everyone to stop writing. Then, she asked the students who sat in front of each row to collect the papers and bring them to her desk. She glanced at them and said, "I will grade these at home and return them to you on Monday."

After recess, we were given a new book with numbers on the front page. Ms. Sedeski said we were going to be learning about arithmetic.

I had never heard the term before so I turned around and asked Geraldine, "What's arithmetic?"

"It's learning how to add and subtract numbers."

I wondered how I was going to do that when I barely knew how to count to ten.

Our teacher said she wanted to share a little rhyme with us before we started to work on our book. She opened a little book and showed us pictures as she read through it. "One, two, buckle my shoe. Three, four, shut the door. Five, six, pick up sticks. Seven, eight, lay them straight. Nine, ten, a big fat hen." The class burst into laughter when she said that.

Ms. Sedeski had a lot of interesting books to share with us. One of them was *Ten Little Indians*. It was a hardcover picture book showing one Indian on the first page, two Indians on the second page, etcetera. She showed us the pictures until she reached the end of the book. Then she said, "I'm going to teach you a little song that will help you remember your numbers, and it goes like this."

She began singing: "One little, two little, three little Indians. Four little, five little, six little Indians. Seven little, eight little, nine little Indians. Ten little Indian boys." She had us sing this song a few times and before we knew it, we could count to ten.

After learning how to count to ten, she had us open our new book to the first page. It said "*Addition*" at the top. She explained our assignment, and I knew this wasn't going to be one of my favourite subjects because I had to use my fingers to count and add the numbers.

I used my eraser a lot during that arithmetic period. When I looked around the room, Maxine and a few others had finished their first page.

They had taken arithmetic before and this was just a review for them.

Before the class ended, Ms. Sedeski told us to hand in our scribblers to the students in the front row. "I will correct your assignments and return them to you on Friday."

The rest of the day went by quickly. The day scholars ran to their buses when school was out; I watched them climb the steps and race to their seats. Oh, how I wished I could go home too.

They were lucky they didn't have to stay here and feel lonely like the rest of us.

I never thought much about prison before, other than what Uncle Ernie talked about, but this was exactly the way he described it.

If we ran away, we would be tracked down by police dogs, brought back here, and punished. It didn't seem fair some students went home while the rest of us had to stay here. Where was the justice in that? Why did we have to stay here locked up? We never did anything wrong.

Then I thought about Uncle Marvin and how I was going to miss him and his cheeky grin.

The following morning, we made our way downstairs and lined up for breakfast. My mouth was sore from a toothache I had earlier that morning. Although most of the ache was gone, my mouth was still tender and I was scared to bite down with that tooth. I was able to eat my porridge, but I had a hard time eating the crust on my toast. I dipped it in milk to make it softer and easier to chew.

As we sat there quietly eating, Sister Andre came to our table and asked, "Have you ever tasted peanut butter and syrup mixed? Try it and let me know what you think."

I decided I would try it after my dental appointment. But for now, I was scared of getting syrup into my sore tooth and ending up with another toothache.

Some of the boys told her it tasted good. She smiled and walked away feeling proud of herself.

After we finished praying and giving thanks for our food, we headed back to our playroom. We sat there while Mr. Gilbert told us about our schedule for the day.

He reminded us of our dental appointments.

I had mixed feelings about mine. I wanted to get my teeth looked at, but I was afraid of the pain at the same time.

"Time for the senior boys to do their chores," Mr. Gilbert said. "The rest of you clean up after yourselves when you use the washroom."

After he finished speaking, we went to the playground.

Someone said, "Hey, you guys, Shanabi is here."

I went to investigate who Shanabi was and several boys were milling around an elderly gentleman who was smiling and talking to them.

Later on, I learned he had a couple of sons who attended school here and had been around Marieval for many years. Most parents didn't have the privilege of visiting their children on the school grounds, but Shanabi was different.

The nuns had raised one of his sons since he was three years old. That's why he would often visit the school.

He lived close by and he would often stop to visit while he was out walking.

I watched as one of the boys gave him a red rubber ball and told him to kick it into the air.

He took that ball and booted it straight up past the roof of that old school.

I had never seen anyone kick a ball so high before. It returned to the cement and bounced back up again. It was fun watching him kick that ball skyward, and I wasn't the only one who thought so. One of the boys retrieved the ball and asked him to kick it again.

We would see him many times after that and we always looked forward to his brief visits.

Everyone around Marieval knew Shanabi and respected him. He would live to be well into his nineties and see the day when Marieval Indian Residential School was shut down in 1975.

(Shanabi) – Photo courtesy of Wapemoose family

Later, we were told to line up for our dental appointments. Sister O'Deil came for us and we followed her to "The Block" then downstairs to the dentist's office. Even before we got to his office, I could smell the local anesthesia that filled the air.

The dentist was an elderly man with a partially balding head. He wore wire-rimmed glasses and a bright white shirt. He smiled at us when we walked into the waiting room and told us to have a seat. He asked who wanted to go first. When no one answered, he pointed to Ernest. "Okay let's start with you." The rest of us breathed a sigh of relief.

We sat there frightened while straining our ears to hear what was going on in the next room. We heard Ernest groan followed by the sound of a drill. For many of us, this was our first visit to a dentist, so we had no idea what to expect.

One by one, the students came out of his office. Some had tears in their eyes while others came out smiling, but nearly everyone had their hands over their mouths.

After what seemed like an eternity, it was my turn to go and sit in his chair. The dentist told me to open my mouth wide as he examined my teeth. He noticed my nervousness and told me to relax, but how could I relax when I was scared stiff? He had a small mirror in one hand and a curved pick in the other. He poked around each tooth before telling me, "You have two cavities that need to be filled immediately."

He turned away and returned with a needle as long as a six-inch ruler and stuck it into my gums while I squirmed around! Back then, they didn't have much in the way of technology, so he didn't use numbing gel or cotton swabs, just horse-sized needles. Then he did the same thing on the inside of my gums and it hurt like nothing I had ever experienced before, and that was only the first tooth. He followed by freezing my second tooth and I could feel tears welling up in my eyes.

Before long, the whole side of my face felt numb. He made sure my gums were frozen before picking up a small round instrument and telling me to keep my mouth open.

I heard the sound of a drill and I could smell smoke in the air. That part didn't hurt as much, but I could feel my toes wiggling around inside my running shoes. Relief flooded through me when he told me I was done. Like some of the other boys, I left his office with my hand over my mouth.

I went back to the playroom where some boys were watching TV. I asked my friend, "Hey, Derek, what's on?"

"It's a Western show called *The Texan*."

I had no idea what the show was about, but I sat there holding my frozen mouth. It didn't take long for the freezing to wear off and the pain to set in. I tasted blood in my mouth, so I went to the washroom and rinsed my mouth with cold water. It still hurt when we went to bed. I didn't feel like talking or reading comics that evening.

When Grandma Smoker saw me holding my mouth, she asked, "Do you have a toothache?"

"I saw a dentist a few hours ago and he gave me two fillings, so my gums are sore."

She reached into one of her drawers and said: "Here. Take these with water." She handed me a couple of aspirin that I quickly washed down with water.

I lay back on my pillow hoping the aspirin would work soon. I fell asleep wondering how many more trips to the dentist I would have to make while I was at Marieval.

As the days passed, I noticed the leaves on the trees was changing colours and the weather was getting colder.

What was Dad doing back home? This was the time of the year he usually cut wood for the winter or went hunting in the park. He liked hunting with Uncle Bill who had extra rifles and was well-equipped for hunting.

They would hunt until they had enough wild meat to feed both of their families during the winter.

The fall weather displayed all the signs nature was getting ready for the cold winter months ahead. The ducks and geese were flocking up for their long migration south.

Grandpa talked to them and wished them a safe journey as they flew overhead. He laughed as he shared how they honked to tell him they would see him again in the spring.

He enjoyed harvesting his garden and filling his root cellar with enough potatoes and vegetables to last through the winter. He always left room for Grandma's canned saskatoons, raspberries, rhubarb, and chokecherries, along with her homemade jams.

During the harvest season, Dad had plenty of work as a hired hand. The wives and daughters cooked large meals for their hungry men. When I ate with them, I felt important sitting at a table stacked with so much food I didn't know where to begin.

On Friday, we went for a walk north of the school where we came to a steel bridge crossing the Qu'Appelle River. It was a very narrow black bridge that was still used by people travelling to a neighbouring town called Grayson.

Mr. Gilbert, said "You can look over the edge but don't climb on it. If you fall off the bridge, you could break some bones, and it will be a long walk back to the school with a broken leg." He laughed at his joke, but we knew what he meant because there were a lot of rocks below the bridge, and it was a long way down.

The smell of rotting fish floated up from the river. A few of them were lying along the riverbank.

We walked along the gravel road until we could see a farmhouse on the right.

Ernest told us the Gerhardt family lived there.

As we climbed a hill, I looked down into a ravine and saw a rabbit running through the bush. It wasn't long before other boys noticed it too. "Sir, may we catch it?"

He said, "Form a large circle so it can't get away."

Some of the boys went around that bush and chased it toward us. We closed the circle and it had nowhere to run. We were certain we were going to catch it. However, at the last second, it raced toward an opening in our circle and it went up the hill and down the other side.

In a way, I was happy it got away. How far would a small rabbit go if we were to all share it for supper? Would the cooks even consider cooking a rabbit for us?

I asked Ernest, "Did you guys ever catch a rabbit on your walks last year?"

"We caught one, but let it go when it started squealing."

Then he turned to Mr. Dennis, "Sir if we caught a rabbit, would we be able to eat it?"

"I'm not sure about any health food concerns, but it wouldn't hurt to ask."

During supper, Mr. Dennis asked the cooks about it.

They laughed and said, "If you catch a rabbit, you'll have to skin and prepare it but we'll cook it for you."

After they said that, my thoughts turned homeward. Our grandparents didn't snare and eat rabbits during the summer.

They only ate them during the winter and stopped hunting them in the spring. There had to be a reason for that.

Saturday was a long lonely day full of memories of my family back home. I didn't stray far from Norman and Ernest all day.

They filled the emptiness for a while, but they couldn't take the place of Mom and Dad.

I dreaded the thought of making a mistake here and getting into trouble, or worse yet, dying and going to hell. But would being in hell be any worse than being stuck here?

That evening we had to take our shower, so I quickly jumped into the damp steaming room and found a spare faucet in the corner. I hurried and lathered myself all over with a bar of soap while keeping an eye out for the supervisors. I was in the process of rinsing the soap out of my hair when Mr. Gilbert came in and made his way to where I was standing.

He stuck my head under the running water and helped me to rinse the soap out my hair before telling me I was done and could get out of the shower.

As I was leaving the room, I noticed he grabbed a junior boy and began scrubbing him with soap. I was glad it wasn't me. Perhaps if I raced into the shower as quickly as possible, I could avoid him in the future.

Later that evening as we went up to our dorm, I noticed Grandma Smoker wasn't there. In her place, a nun introduced herself as Sister David, then told us to change into our pyjamas and brush our teeth.

When we used the sinks in the junior boys' dorm, the smaller boys were not bullied like they were downstairs. We were courteous and everyone was given an equal opportunity to use the washroom on a first-come, first-served basis.

After everyone was finished in the washroom, Sister David told us to kneel by our beds while she prayed and encouraged us to pray along with her.

After we finished praying, I sat on Ernest's bed and listened to him talking about the day's events. I was looking at one of the walls and asked him "Do you know what's in the next room?"

"It's a small chapel. The nuns and priests sometimes go in there to say their rosary in the evenings and early mornings. The room next to that is the nursing station, so if you ever need to see the nurse, that's where you go."

Soon the lights blinked and As I climbed into bed, the lights went out. I couldn't sleep right away, so I watched Sister David by the dim light of the exit sign. She sat in the dark, praying with her rosary.

Chapter 3 - We Just Want to Go Home

Early Sunday morning, I woke to the sound of muffled footsteps in the dorm. A nun was opening a locked closet and removing clothes from the shelves. She placed a white shirt and grey dress pants at the foot of my bed.

I peeked at her as she put dress clothes at the foot of everyone's bed. Were these the clothes I would be wearing to go home? I was excited at the thought of leaving this place. I couldn't wait for the supervisor to turn on the lights and tell us we were going home.

As we made our beds, I saw Norman, and said, "I think we're going home. It's sure going to be nice to see Mom and Dad again."

Norman was excited too as we made our way downstairs to the playroom. He smiled at me as we sat on the benches.

Then both supervisors came in. They said, "We will be going to Mass in a few minutes." So, instead of going home, we were going to church. What a bitter disappointment!

I can't explain the helplessness and pity I felt for Norman. Just a few minutes ago, he was happy to be going home, but now he looked like he wanted to cry. I was so disappointed and angry at this place for making my brother cry.

Some of the junior boys had red eyes, and I knew they were crying too. If I didn't have to worry about my brother then life here would've been so much easier. In a way, I was happy we were together, but on the other hand, it was difficult to see him cry. When were we going home?

My thoughts were interrupted by a supervisor telling us to line up in two rows. We walked up the cement steps and out the door past the parlour.

I could hear the lonely sound of a church bell ringing as we made our way to the service. There were a few boys ahead of me, but most of them were behind.

We must have looked like a large family of penguins following one another on our way to the sea.

As we entered the church, Sister David stood by a silver bowl containing a sponge and water. "Before you go and sit in the pews, or enter for catechism classes, wet your fingers in the holy water and bless yourselves by making a sign of the cross. You will do this every time you enter the church." She whispered to the newcomers, "There will be no talking or fooling around in church and only the ones who have received their First Communion can go up and receive Communion."

After we blessed ourselves, the junior boys, which included the grade-one class, were taken to the church basement for catechism classes. We were introduced to a tall white lady who said, "While in class, you may call me Ms. Lang or teacher."

She was going to share stories from the Bible and we were going to play games while the Mass was going on upstairs. She read stories from a hardcover book with a lot of interesting pictures in it.

Then she gave us pictures to colour and cut out. This was new to me, and I was glad to be doing something interesting. But I was still disappointed at the thought of not going home.

The service upstairs lasted for about an hour. I couldn't tell the time yet, but eventually, we were dismissed and the girls left the church first.

They filed out in two rows and returned to their playroom.

When we returned to our playroom, Mr. Gilbert informed us we were going back to the church for a High Mass service. We would not be changing out of our Sunday clothes until that service was over. We were getting hungry. Were we ever going to have breakfast? We waited patiently for the dining bell to ring. This would be our signal to line up for breakfast.

When the bell finally rang, we entered the dining room.

The girls were sitting there with food in front of them. Why did they have the privilege of doing everything first?

I saw my cousin Shirley in the dining room and she waved and smiled when she saw me. Of course, I didn't know it at the time, but Shirley and John were flirting with one another. That was the reason he was so protective.

He wanted to stay on Shirley's good side. However, he was such a nice guy he would have looked after us anyway.

After wolfing down a breakfast of warm lumpy porridge, dry toast, a slice of bologna, and a cup of milk, our supervisors told us were going back to the church.

I didn't know the difference between a High Mass and a Low Mass service because we went downstairs for catechism lessons.

This time our teacher was Sister Mary, and she kept us downstairs for about thirty minutes. She gave us blue plastic fluorescent rosaries and told us they would glow in the dark. She explained about the different prayers each bead represented. Then she said we were going upstairs to join the Mass already in progress.

During the Mass, a nun came over to the front pew and told us to stand up, kneel, or sit down like everyone else. It seemed like we were always in the wrong position, so I learned to peek behind me and see what the other boys were doing. If they were kneeling or sitting down, that is what I would do so the nun didn't have to come over and correct us.

The High Mass was longer than the Low Mass. The priest prayed and chanted in a strange language.

I learned later on the strange language, Latin, was often used in High Mass. During the service, I grew drowsy as Father Dumont read his sermon. I had a hard time keeping my eyes open.

Someone poked me from behind and told me to wake up.

When I glanced back, it was Mr. Gilbert and I hoped I wasn't in trouble.

The priest's sermon was a long one as he shared stories from the Bible about how Christ lived his life.

As he spoke, I glanced around the church and stared at some pictures on the walls. One that caught my attention was of a man hanging from a cross, similar to the cross we had on our rosary. Why was that done to him? It looked like someone put nails in his hands and feet while putting a crown of thorns on his head. Boy, that must have hurt.

I once walked through a thorn bush back home and knew how much those thorns hurt. Some bad people must have done this to him. Maybe Ernest knows about it. I'll ask him later to see what he says.

When the service was over, I watched the altar boys go downstairs to the basement of the church. They wore long red cassocks instead of the black ones they had worn earlier.

I couldn't help but stare at two of them because I had seen them somewhere before, but I couldn't remember where. Then it dawned on me: those were the two boys who were riding their bikes from Mr. Lang's house.

When we left the church, we walked back to our playroom and were sent to our dorm to change into our regular clothes. Our clothes were more like uniforms because everyone was dressed alike. The only way to distinguish our clothes from the others was by the numbers sewn into the back of them.

While we were upstairs, I asked Ernest, "When are we going home?"

"Not until Christmas," he said.

"What is Christmas? When is it?" We didn't celebrate Christmas back home.

He said, "Christmas is about three months away. That's when Santa Claus will come."

As he spoke, I wondered who was going to set rabbit snares and bring home the rabbits for Grandma. I missed our home and hated this place.

Later that evening as we sat on the floor in the playroom with the rest of the junior boys, we watched an episode of *The Ed Sullivan Show*. There were a variety of performers on this show. Some of them were singers, some were circus performers, some were magicians, and others were comedians. I liked the comedians because they were funny and made me laugh. Laughter made me forget about my loneliness for a little while.

As we sat there watching the show, Ernest whispered to us, "I hope they let us stay up for *Bonanza*. It comes on at nine o'clock."

I asked him, "What kind of show is *Bonanza*?"

"It's a good cowboy show."

We sat with our fingers crossed when *The Ed Sullivan Show* ended, hoping we wouldn't be sent to bed before *Bonanza* started. It must have worked because Mr. Gilbert said, "Right after *Bonanza;* everyone will be going to bed."

This was the first time I watched this show and it kept me riveted to the television. All the lights in the playroom were turned off except for a small red lamp in the shape of a miniature covered wagon. It glowed at the top of the television.

As I watched *Bonanza,* I noticed how cool Little Joe looked and wished I could be like him; he rode a nice black-and-white pinto horse.

All the boys were silent. It was an unwritten rule there would be no talking until the commercials came on. You could have heard a pin drop in the room, yet there was excitement in the air as the drama unfolded. There was a sigh of relief as the Cartwrights got themselves out of danger. At the end of the show, there was a preview of what was going to happen next week. It was a good way to end our day, and it became a regular television show we all looked forward to watching on Sunday evenings.

At ten o'clock, we went up to the dorm, still whispering about the parts of *Bonanza* we liked. After we put on our pyjamas and brushed our teeth, we knelt by our beds and said our prayers for the night.

Even though it was late, Grandma Smoker allowed us a half-hour to read our comics before turning out the lights for the night.

That night, I dreamt I was back home playing with my younger brother, Oranges. He showed me a tree on the north side of our shack he could climb on. A path went by Grandma's clothesline and down into a small ravine we called "*the hollow*" and that is where he was playing.

I told him to be careful as he made his way up a tree. While he was climbing it, I noticed an old rotten log on the ground, so I rolled it over and spotted a big garter snake hiding beneath it.

She had several baby snakes with her, and when she opened her mouth, all the baby snakes crawled inside.

I remembered that dream when the lights came on the next morning.

Mom always took the time to listen to me no matter how trivial my questions were. This school was so cold and indifferent. Thinking about my dream made me lonely.

I wished I was back home spending time with my younger brother and making slingshots with Norman. I longed for the hot days of summer exploring nature and being in the bush.

As we lined up for a class on Monday, I saw Burl holding his ear, so I asked him, "What's wrong with your ear?"

"I have an earache."

When I looked at his ear, it was red and looked infected. An ugly smell came from it. I didn't know much about ear problems, but something was wrong and I needed to tell someone. So, during class, I went to our teacher's desk. I told her, "Burl has an earache. Can you please have a look at it?"

Ms. Sedeski called him to the front and examined his ear. She looked frightened and told the class she would be right back as she took Burl's hand and disappeared down the hall.

She came back a few minutes later, but she was alone and didn't tell us what happened.

I didn't see Burl for a couple of days after that. There was a rumour going around he had been taken to the hospital in Broadview.

While he was gone, we received our arithmetic assignments back. Because of a couple of mistakes in mine, I didn't get a gold star, but Norman had one on his page and he made sure I knew about it.

"I guess I'm smarter in arithmetic than you are," he said and he was right. Arithmetic was not one of my favourite subjects, but I liked reading about Dick and Jane and their adventures.

In one of the stories, their younger sister Sally had the mumps. At the time I didn't know mumps was real, but it was an illness that would later come to Marieval.

After our first recess, Ms. Sedeski returned our tests where we had identified the objects in the pictures. I noticed a gold star on my sheet with a comment: Very good. Wow! I got them all right!

When we had some spare time, I went to the back of the classroom and showed my work to Norman. "What did you get on your paper?" I asked him.

"I got them all right." He showed me his gold star too.

I wanted to show off my star, so I went to see my friend Richard who had a silver star on his page. I said, "A silver star is almost as good as a gold one."

During class, I was preoccupied with assignments and school brought out my competitive spirit. I wanted to get gold stars and be smart. However, some of the pictures in the books reminded me of home and made me lonesome. Would things ever be the same for us back home on White Bear?

There were so many rules here, so many things to remember, and the constant fear of making a mistake and getting yelled at. You had to avoid some of the senior boys because they liked to bully the younger ones and make them cry. At least in class, there was a refuge from the bullies, and the rules were a little more relaxed.

Our teacher rarely yelled. Most of the time it happened when she was singing at the top of her voice. When she liked a song, she cranked the volume up on her little record player. Sometimes she got a bit carried away singing; that's when the yelling came in.

After supper, the supervisors gave us a choice to play outside or watch *The Three Stooges* on television. I never saw this show before, so I stayed in to watch it.

Some of the boys found it hilarious and laughed at the three stooges named Larry, Curly, and Moe, who kept getting themselves into all kinds of hilarious predicaments. To make matters worse they were always slapping one another for being stupid and it looked funny.

When the show was over, I went outside to look for Norman and Ernest.

Out on the playground, Mr. Dennis batted softballs into the air while some of the boys wearing baseball gloves played a game of five hundred. For every high fly they caught, they would get one hundred points. Balls caught on the first bounce were worth fifty points, while grounders were worth twenty-five points.

I decided to give it a try and picked out a glove. Everyone kept track of their scores and the first one to reach five hundred points became the next batter. It was fun, but I could only catch the ones rolling on the ground because the senior boys pushed me off the way when a high fly was coming towards us. They would call it and say, "It's mine!" or "I got it!" and force me to get out of the way.

I waited patiently for a high fly to come my way. When it did, I shouted, "I got it!" I put my glove up in the air and watched the ball coming towards it, but somehow it missed my glove and hit me right between my eyes. I fell to the ground writhing in pain and could hear voices asking me if I was okay, but I wasn't.

I went back to the playroom in tears. I wished Mom was here to help me like she always did whenever I got hurt.

She had a way with words and always knew how to make the hurt go away. She never told me to stop crying or to stop being a sissy. She let me have a good cry and held me while she offered words of comfort and encouragement.

I spent the rest of the evening sitting on a bench holding my swollen face.

The supervisors never asked how I was feeling. They could have sent me to the school nurse for medication to deal with the throbbing pain but that never happened.

When I looked in the mirror, I could see two shiners that made me look like a raccoon. My left eye was bruised and swollen shut. My right eye was also bruised but I could see light and movement through it.

Later that evening, I didn't feel like watching TV or doing anything. For once, I was happy we were going to bed.

When we were in the small boys' dorm some of the boys pulled out their comics. Ernest had a few and asked, "Do you guys want to read one?"

I asked him what kind of comics he had and he showed us *Superman, Kid Colt Outlaw,* and *The Rawhide Kid.* I let Norman choose first and I was glad when he picked *Superman* because I liked reading the Western ones.

I squinted at the pictures and was halfway through my comic when the lights went out. Of course, I couldn't read yet, but I could follow the story by looking at the pictures. I was tempted to finish reading it in the washroom, but I knew if I got caught, I would be in trouble.

Before I fell asleep, I looked at my new rosary under the blankets and it lit up like a firefly. I smiled and played with it for a while.

After a few minutes, I saw Norman going to the washroom. I got out of bed and followed him in there. "Norman, I'm lonesome," I whispered a little too loudly.

"Shh. Talk quietly so Grandma Smoker won't hear you."

I lowered my voice. "Do you think Mom and Dad are coming to get us for Christmas?"

"I'm sure they won't just leave us here."

I was hoping he was right, but I asked, "What if they can't make it? Then we'll be stuck here forever." Boy, that was a scary thought.

That night I felt sorry for some newcomers who were crying themselves to sleep. Their sniffling and sobbing said they were hurt and lonely. I knew how they felt. I wondered how much longer we would have to stay here as I thought about my family back home.

The next morning, my face was still swollen. There were black and purple marks around both of my eyes. The way some of the girls stared at me during breakfast made my face turn red. To them, it probably looked like someone had given me a good beating.

I kept my head down while we were in the dining room and listened to John as he talked about a cliff, he called the cut bank. It sounded like a dangerous place and I wasn't sure if I wanted to go there.

He said, "The last time we went there for a walk we were allowed to climb down that cliff while a supervisor watched from above. It was too steep for him to climb down with us."

One of the boys asked, "Weren't you afraid of falling?"

"Nah. I'm used to climbing the hills around the school. I grew up around here, and I'm not afraid of scaling the cut bank." He laughed. "I was born in a wagon on a steep grade on Kahkewistahaw reserve. Maybe that is why I'm not afraid of climbing hills."

From the school, the hills looked very high. I wasn't too crazy about climbing to the top of them. Oh well, that was something I would worry about when the time came.

After breakfast, Mr. Gilbert said, "Friday, everyone will be receiving a vaccine to prevent the spread of tuberculosis. You'll be scheduled to meet with the medical team, starting with the grade-one students. I realize some of you received your shots last year, but the principal said all medical records are to be reviewed to ensure they are up-to-date."

After he finished speaking, Ernest said he remembered getting a needle for T.B. last year.

He said, "It didn't hurt, but some boys had complications last year."

Norman looked concerned, "What kind of complications are you talking about?"

"A couple of boys got infected and had to be treated by the school nurse." To prove his point, he showed us a scar on his right arm.

After looking at his scar, I realized this was no ordinary needle and some pain must have been involved.

On Friday morning, we followed Mr. Gilbert to the gym to receive our shots. Our female classmates were ahead of us, so we were told to form another line for our x-rays.

I never received an x-ray before, so I wasn't sure if I should believe Ernest when he told me it didn't hurt. I kept my eyes on a couple of boys ahead of me to see if there were any signs of pain on their faces. It was painless.

I was relieved when I was done in that line and told to go to the other one for a tuberculosis shot. This is the part that concerned me because I didn't like needles.

When it was my turn, I turned my head away so I couldn't see what was happening. Before I knew it, I was done. It didn't hurt as much as the needles I received from the dentist.

When we were back in class, Ms. Sedeski told us a story about Christopher Columbus, who discovered America.

He was an early explorer who was searching for India and accidentally came over here. He thought he was in India, so he called us Indians and that name stuck.

She told us about their first *Thanksgiving* and how it became an annual celebration. This was new to me because I couldn't remember my family celebrating *Thanksgiving* back home on White Bear.

Ms. Sedeski gave us an assignment to colour pictures of turkeys, Pilgrims, and Indians standing around a table full of food. All that food looked good and made me feel hungry.

When we were finished colouring, our teacher had us cut out our pictures and tape them to the windows as decorations for *Thanksgiving*. She told us there would be no school on Monday because it was a statutory holiday. Happiness lit the faces of the day scholars.

I couldn't share their joy because I wasn't going home for the long weekend. There wasn't very much to be thankful for in this place. If we were going home, then we could celebrate and be happy like the Indians in the pictures we coloured, cut out, and taped to the windows.

The weekend went by slowly. Saturday, Mr. Dennis said, "We're going for a walk toward the cut bank."

Now I would get a chance to see what it looked like and maybe even climb down that cliff I heard so much about. I could hardly wait to get there.

As we walked by an old house, I saw Ning-Ning talking to someone who was sitting outside on his porch.

Ernest said, "The old man is Ning-Ning's uncle. Everyone calls him Don Mathew. He's one of the night watchmen at the school and he's famous for his tall tales. If one of the boys thinks you're lying or telling a fib, they'll say, 'Stop pulling a Don Mathew' and laugh at you."

I never did meet him in person, but I probably saw him passing through the senior boys' dorm the few nights we slept there. I would see him many times after that sitting on his porch whenever we went for walks by his place.

After arriving at the cut bank, I looked down and saw how steep it was; it was much steeper than I had imagined.

Some boys made their way down toward the creek while Mr. Dennis and a few junior boys stayed at the top.

After giving it considerable thought, I decided to go for it. I found a place where I could inch my way downward. It only took a few minutes for me to be hopelessly stuck along a steep wall, too afraid to look down. Both of my hands were glued to the cliff, and I couldn't move for fear of falling the rest of the way down that steep embankment.

I thought about it for a few minutes then let one of my hands go and slowly turned around so I was facing the direction I came from. What a relief! Now I could inch myself back up the cliff.

Once I reached the top, I sat on the ground. I wasn't going to do that again.

We continued our walk up to another high hill and I was too scared to look down.

I had to crawl on my hands and knees to keep from falling backward, and it was hard keeping up with the rest of the boys. I tried not to look down because it was too high and heights terrified me. I was happy when I reached the top of the hill. I could see the school and the surrounding buildings from that vantage point.

We rested for a while before heading back. A trail wound down the hill, and some of the boys ran down the trail. Why didn't we use this trail to get to the top? It would've made climbing the hill a whole lot easier. Maybe we climbed it for a test of our endurance. Maybe it was for the exercise because it sure had my adrenaline going.

At school, the days turned into weeks, and eventually, it seemed like we were here forever. I was beginning to think Mom and Dad had forgotten about us. So, I was surprised one day when Norman and I received a letter from home.

Father Carriere came to our playroom and handed out some mail to the boys.

I didn't pay much attention until he called out Norman's name and told him he had received a letter from home.

He told Norman he had opened the letter to check the contents. I'm not sure what he was looking for in our mail, so I assumed if he opened the letter, then he read it too.

When Norman opened the letter, he said, "It's from Mom." It was a bit of a struggle for us, but eventually, we were able to sound out the words and read the letter.

Mom told us Dad found a job near Brooks, Alberta, and was working on a cattle ranch. He loved his job because he rode horses every day and worked with cattle. Sometimes, the rancher's wife would hire her to do some housecleaning. It was a large ranch with a bunkhouse, guest house, and the main house, so there was a lot of work for them.

As Norman did his best to read the letter, I peeked into the envelope and saw money inside! When he pulled it out, he discovered Mom and Dad sent us each six dollars! We were rich and we didn't know how we were going to spend all that money.

When Mr. Dennis noticed our money, he asked, "Do you boys want to keep your money in an account?"

Norman told him, "No, that's okay."

We rarely had money so this was like walking around with gold in our pockets.

Ernest said, "You guys are lucky to have money. There's an annual bazaar coming soon."

"What happens at the bazaar?"

"The community hall will be decorated with many tables that are filled with food, crafts, toys, and games. Why don't you ask if we can go to Mr. Leost's store?"

Norman told him, "No, you ask. If they let us go to the store, you can come with us."

I crossed my fingers as I heard Ernest say, "Sir, Norman and Walter want to know if they can take me to the store?"

It wasn't a usual practice to let school boarders go to the store because it was outside of the school boundaries. So, we weren't surprised when a supervisor said, "No."

There was no preferential treatment at Marieval and this was proof of that. But it didn't stop me from thinking of my newfound wealth. I sat in the playroom thinking of all the candies and goodies in that convenience store.

The store was owned by Mr. Leost, a senior gentleman with white hair and thick black glasses. The last time I saw him in church, he wore a white shirt and baggy pants with suspenders holding them up, the same kind Grandpa always wore. Images of all the goodies in his store danced in my head, and I realized I was only dreaming because we weren't allowed to go there.

We woke up one autumn morning and Ernest said, "Today we can go to the bazaar."

I had never been to one before, so I didn't know what to expect. Before we left our playroom, we were reminded of the rules we were to follow while we were there. As usual, we lined up outside before marching to the hall in two rows.

We entered the community hall, and the many sights and sounds amazed us. The smell of popcorn filled the room and we could hear numbers being called at a bingo. All kinds of food were for sale, and tables were filled with different crafts and toys on display.

"Let's go see that fish pond in the corner." I pointed to a sign: *Try your luck for 10 cents*. The game looked like it was a lot of fun, and it didn't take much to convince Norman to follow me.

When we got to the fish pond, Sister Andre was standing beside a table. Her job was to collect a dime in exchange for a small wooden fishing rod. Then she let us cast our rod behind a white sheet where someone put a toy on the fishing rod. Next, we had to pull back the fishing rod and see what we caught.

I caught a bag of marbles and Norman caught a cap gun.

We gave Ernest a dime and told him to give it a try.

He was fishing out his prize when Sister Andre stopped it and went behind the sheet.

After talking with someone, she told Ernest to try it again. She laughed when he revealed his prize. It was a new comic, but according to her, he almost snagged a doll. That would have been funny to see.

The smell of fresh popcorn was making me hungry, so I looked around and discovered it was coming from a corner of the hall. I told Norman and Ernest I wanted to buy a bag of popcorn and they should come along if they wanted some. I was surprised when I got there and saw my teacher selling popcorn.

She smiled and said, "Hi, Walter, would you like to try some hot buttery popcorn?"

I nodded and reached for my change.

She asked "Do you want a small bag or a large one? The small bags cost five cents, and the larger bags cost ten cents."

That hot popcorn sure smelled good, so I bought a large bag. I was going to ask Norman and Ernest if they wanted some, but when I turned around, they were gone.

I lost them somewhere in the crowd, so I wandered around to the different tables. One was selling new and used comics. The new ones were in transparent plastic bags. The used ones didn't have plastic covers, but they were laid out in neat little rows. There were so many comics to choose from I didn't know where to begin.

As I surveyed the table, I stared at a large cardboard sign with the prices marked on it. New comics cost twelve cents and used ones sold for ten cents apiece or three for a quarter. I bought *Kid Colt Outlaw*, *The Rawhide Kid*, and *The Lone Ranger*. While looking through my comics and eating popcorn, I saw Richard standing by himself with his hands in his pockets. "Hey, Richard! Come check out this table!"

He smiled. "I would, but I don't have any money."

"I still have some money left. Why don't you pick out a few comics? We'll swap after we're done reading them."

A smile lit up his face. "Okay. I'll pay you back the next time I have money."

When we were done at this table, we decided to look around the bazaar some more. We talked to a lady who was selling beaded moccasins, mittens, and baby clothes.

She told us she made all of her handicraft items and had been coming to this bazaar for a few years. She looked around the room before whispering, "I get a lot of my business from setting up booths at pow-wows."

I wanted to buy a beaded wristband, but Richard said, "You won't be able to wear it. It's different and the supervisors will most likely take it away from you."

Yeah, he was probably right. I didn't think I had enough money for it anyway.

After talking with her for a while, we walked around some more and came across a table where a man was selling straw baskets that contained different kinds of apples, along with oranges, bananas, and purple grapes. The baskets were nicely decorated with coloured cellophane wrap. One probably would have made a nice gift for a family. The baskets didn't interest me because I received fruit for lunch every afternoon and didn't have to pay for it.

A man was shouting for people to try their luck at a game of *Crown & Anchor*, so we decided to go and give it a try. We placed our quarters down and the man gave the wheel a big spin. The wheel spun around while making a clicking sound. We crossed our fingers as the wheel slowed down and eventually came to a halt, but it didn't stop on any of the squares where we had placed our bets, so we lost our money.

I was thinking of trying it again, but Richard coaxed me into leaving before we lost any more money. Once again, I knew he was right.

At the next table, a vendor was selling hot dogs, hamburgers, and pop. I asked my friend if he was hungry.

He nodded and smiled at me.

We looked at the prices which were marked for everyone to see. Hotdogs were cheaper than hamburgers but not as filling, so we both ordered a hamburger and a bottle of pop.

We sat at an empty picnic table to eat our lunch when my friend pointed to a table where they were selling ice cream. We smiled at one another as the ice cream looked tempting.

After we finished eating our hamburgers, we went over to the booth where a nice lady was selling ice-cream cones.

She smiled and asked, "Would you like some ice cream?"

We said in unison, "Yes, we would!"

"Do you want one scoop or two? And what flavours would you like?"

I asked for two scoops of strawberry and Richard wanted two scoops of chocolate. It was a nice treat and I couldn't remember the last time I had an ice-cream cone. "Hey, Pal, when was the last time you had an ice-cream cone?"

He smiled and said he couldn't remember.

After we finished eating our ice-cream, we went outside to look for some of our friends.

Before long, we heard laughter coming from behind the hall. Out of curiosity, we went to check it out, and that's where we found Ernest and Norman. They were sitting on top of a small ledge with some senior boys and girls.

A couple of the boys had their arms around some girls who were laughing and giggling. That's when I noticed John and my cousin Shirley sitting up there.

When she saw me, Shirley smiled and said, "There's my little cousin."

Some of the boys were smoking and one of them asked, "Do you guys want a smoke?"

Shirley quickly spoke up. "He's too young to smoke. Don't you dare give him one."

I told Richard, "We should get out of here before one of the supervisors or nuns comes around the corner and catches everyone smoking. Then, we'll all be in trouble."

Norman asked me. "Where did you buy your comics?"

"There's a table inside with a lot of comics for sale."

Upon hearing this, he raced into the hall with Ernest following close behind him.

Richard and I caught up to them as they were rummaging through the piles of comics.

Ernest asked Norman if he could buy two of them called *Robin Hood* and *Tarzan*.

Norman replied, "Sure. Put them on top of my comics and I'll pay for them." There were so many to choose from and most of them were brand new with the sticker prices still on them. After carefully selecting the ones he wanted, Norman asked the young man "How much do I owe you?"

The owner added up the bill and said, "That will be one dollar and twenty-five cents. Enjoy reading them."

Norman and Ernest both smiled as the young man put their comics into a bag.

The rest of the afternoon at the bazaar went by quickly. Before we knew it, we were told to line up outside the hall and we walked back to our playroom. My tummy was full from eating all that food at the bazaar, so I hoped we wouldn't be given too much for supper.

Once we were in the dining room, I asked if anyone wanted the two boiled eggs on my plate and one of the senior boys quickly snatched them up.

Norman didn't eat as much as I did at the bazaar, so he was happy when I gave him my dessert. For milk, I took half a cup and managed to eat the rest of the food on my plate.

The weather was getting colder, and the fierce winds that whipped through the valley were hard on our faces and exposed skin. Because of the harsh weather, the supervisors issued us parkas, long johns, woollen socks, earmuffs, mitts, and winter boots.

The junior boys, like me, had our mitts tied together by a string that ran through our coat sleeves. We were also given woollen toques to keep our heads and ears warm.

Most of the senior boys preferred earmuffs because the toques messed up their hair.

Sometimes we were sent outside even though the weather was brutally cold. We had a dressing room, but it was locked because the skating rink wasn't ready yet.

One day I went outside, and the playground was deserted. I roamed around and found some boys huddled in a corner near the dressing room. When I joined them, I was on the outside of the group and I could still feel the cold wind.

I went inside to use the washroom. If I took my time, I would be warm for a while. But that didn't last long because one of the senior boys told me to hurry up. After all, he still had to clean the toilets.

I was still cold when I went outside and didn't know where to go to fight off the chill. I stood outside the door and heard laughter coming from close by. So, I peeked around the corner and saw some boys standing by an air vent. It was the perfect place to seek shelter because the vent was blowing warm air. I joined the boys and before long, I was warm again. I knew this area was off-limits and if we were caught here, we'd be chased back into the cold.

Chapter 4 - The Lonely Fall Season

The cold weather meant the staff and senior boys would soon be flooding the rink. But that seemed like such a long time to wait, so some of the boys asked the supervisors if they could go skating on the river like they did last year.

Mr. Gilbert said, "First, I'll check the ice to see if it is thick enough to go skating on."

When he returned, he said, "The ice should be okay in a few days. There are still a few spots where the ice is a bit thin, but if we're careful, we should be alright."

Saturday, we were given skates from the white building, which was located next to the main building. Our skates were old with rusty blades and soft toes, but that didn't matter. We were excited about getting away from this prison and doing something different for a while.

Most of the boys knew how to skate, so when my friends asked me if I knew how to skate, I didn't know what to say.

I remember watching Dad skate on a slough back home. It didn't look that hard. But watching someone skate and skating myself were two different things as I was about to find out.

As we went to the river with our skates strapped over our shoulders, I noticed a couple of the boys who didn't have skates like the rest of us did. That seemed kind of odd.

I asked one of them, "Why aren't you going to skate?"

"I'm not allowed because I have athlete's foot. It's contagious and whoever wears the skates after me could catch it. So, until the health nurse okays it, I'm not allowed."

When we arrived at the riverbank, a supervisor showed us the areas to avoid where the ice was still too thin to skate on. The unsafe areas were marked for everyone to see.

As we sat among the bulrushes putting on our skates, Ernest told me to tie my skate laces as tight as possible so my ankles wouldn't wobble around.

I tried to get them as tight as I could, but when I stood up, I was very unsteady. Things got worse when I stepped onto the ice. One foot went one way and the other foot went in another direction. I fell on my face and looked around to see if anyone was watching.

Then I heard someone laughing. When I looked up, I saw a few girls standing along the riverbank watching me.

They wanted to skate too, so their supervisor brought them down to the river to skate with us. In a way, it was nice to have them with us, but it would have been so much better if I knew how to skate so they wouldn't laugh at my expense.

We had a lot of fun on the river that afternoon.

Norman caught on quickly and didn't fall as often as I did. He told me to watch him and he would glide a long way.

I didn't feel too bad about falling when some junior girls couldn't skate very well either.

Most of the senior boys could skate fast and stop quickly just like our dad did back home.

I watched one of them skating forward, backward, and sideways. It was exciting to watch him cruise around.

He flew by the other skaters and made his way from one part of the river to the next. He came around some bulrushes, and before I knew it, he fell into the river with a big splash. His arms waved frantically and his feet were kicking so he could stay above the water.

The supervisors must have heard the splash too because it didn't take them long to come and investigate what was happening. They helped him out of the water, and he was shaking like a leaf from the cold.

His clothes were wet from top to bottom, and he looked very cold as he sat on the riverbank removing his skates.

Mr. Gilbert asked, "Why were you skating there when you knew the ice was too thin?"

"I tried to turn when I rounded the corner, but I lost my balance and fell through the ice."

Mr. Gilbert told him to go back to the school and ask one of the staff for a dry set of clothes. He also told him to spend the rest of the afternoon there because his skates were wet.

At four o'clock that afternoon, the whistle blew and it was time to go back to the school. Skating was an awesome way to spend a Saturday afternoon. While having fun, we forgot about being lonely for our parents back home. This was the first time many of us had ever been on skates, so we had a new experience to share with our families the next time we went home for the holidays.

Back at the school, we returned our skates to the office. The office had doors that were divided in half so the bottom half could remain shut while the top half opened. It was through one of these doors that a supervisor received our skates and gave us back our shoes. Anytime we wanted to go skating after that, we had to get permission and ask for our skates while they kept our boots in the office.

The following day, I noticed some changes on the playground. It all began when I saw a tractor pulling a wagonload of boards along with a few rolls of wire and wooden posts.

Some staff members and senior boys began to pound the posts into the ground while laying boards next to the posts.

I sat on the swings close to where they worked and watched them.

Ernest said, "They're putting up our skating rink. Now that the cold weather is here, it won't be long before we'll be skating and playing hockey. There are going to be two rinks on our side. One rink will be for the senior boys and one for the junior boys. But only the senior boys' rink will have boards around it while the junior boys' rink will only have a sheet of ice for skating. The girls are also going to have a rink on their side, but we won't be allowed to skate there."

Before long, I could see the rink on our side starting to take shape. I watched hockey on television, so I had an idea what a skating rink looked like. It didn't take them more than a couple of days to have all the boards in place, and we waited for them to start flooding the ice. A long black hose extended from the dressing room to the rink. Lights on lampposts around the rink made it possible to flood the ice after dark. We would also be able to use the rink for hockey games and skating parties once the daylight was gone.

The supervisors and a couple of senior boys flooded the rink for a few days. Now there was a nice layer of ice on the ground; it was almost ready for skating.

Excitement filled the air as the supervisors posted a list of hockey teams on our bulletin board. They also posted a schedule of league games which included visiting teams from Lebret, Neudorf, Grayson, Grenfell, and Broadview.

We were told to stay off the ice until it was ready for skating, but we could use the dressing room to warm up when it was cold outside.

I liked the small dressing room, which was furnished with benches around the room and a heater in the centre. There were also shelves placed along the walls that held hockey equipment of all shapes and sizes.

Our skates were in varying conditions. The junior boys' worn-out skates had soft toes, which didn't offer us much protection if we got shot on the foot.

One day I was sitting in the dressing room, and listening to a conversation about hockey last season. One of the boys said, "I heard helmets and goalie masks are going to become mandatory for players in the National Hockey League. Right now, helmets aren't mandatory maybe that's why we only have two old helmets in the dressing room."

As their conversation continued, I examined the hockey gloves. They were in poor shape. Most of them had holes in the palms and thumb areas. Several old goalie pads were also in the dressing room. It looked like whoever was in goal could wear a wire mask, the kind baseball catchers used.

Most of the hockey sticks had cracked or chipped blades and were held together by black hockey tape.

As the boys spoke, I watched Garry carve his initials into a puck so no one could claim it. I thought that was a good idea and I would remember it when I got a puck of my own.

Although the junior boys' rink didn't have boards it was big enough for a couple of nets and a good game of shinny. That small rink would come in handy when the senior boys were using the big rink for hockey practice or scheduled games. It was a good idea for the junior boys to have their ice surface to avoid getting hit by flying pucks or run over by the senior players.

The following Saturday, our ice still wasn't ready, so we went skating on the river again. This time there wouldn't be any girls to see me flop around on the ice. One of the boys asked a supervisor if we could take sticks and pucks to the river for a game of hockey.

Mr. Dennis thought it was a good idea, so upon our arrival at the river, the boys chose teams. Needless to say, I wasn't much of a hockey player. I used a hockey stick to hold myself up. It seemed like I was chasing the puck one way when everyone was coming back the other way.

Eventually, they asked me to play goal, which was marked by two rocks on the ice. I spent most of my time on my knees to keep the puck out. I was standing in goal when one of the boys had a breakaway and shot the puck at me. The puck hit my toes where my skates were wet and soft. It hurt so much I rolled around on the ice and cried. The frozen puck hurt my cold foot and I didn't want to play anymore.

After limping to the riverbank, I removed my skates so I could rub my toes. My socks were wet and my feet cold. Before long, the supervisor's whistle blew and we knew it was time to walk back to the school.

Mr. Gilbert said, "If we keep flooding the ice, it should be ready for skating by the weekend." And sure enough, it was ready.

We had our first skating party scheduled for Saturday night. We were told the girls would be joining us for an hour, and we were to be respectful and on our best behaviour while they were on our side. Anyone caught being disrespectful would be reprimanded and sent to our playroom.

I had never been to a skating party before so I asked, "Ernest, what happens at a skating party?"

"It's a lot of fun. The girls come to our side and skate with us. Some boys skate with the girls and hold their hands while skating around to music played over a loudspeaker. The junior boys play frozen tag and have races."

At the skating party, I didn't know how to skate very well, but I was okay if I held onto the boards. I could cruise along and skate a short distance before I lost my balance and fell.

Shirley asked me to skate with her. She held my hand and kept grabbing me whenever I was going to fall. She laughed as my wobbly ankles made short strides and I tried not to fall. It took us a while but we made it around the rink a couple of times before I told her I was tired. She brought me to the dressing room so I could have a rest and warm up.

When I returned to the rink, I watched a few senior boys and girls holding hands while gliding around the ice. There were also supervisors, Father Carriere and a nun, who were skating around and enjoying themselves.

Some of the intermediate boys were racing around and showing off their speed skating skills to the girls.

I envied them and hoped I would be able to skate as fast as them someday.

When the skating party was over, our supervisors thanked the girls for coming over and told them we had a very nice time. It only lasted for an hour but we were already looking forward to the next one.

Before they left, Shirley hugged me and thanked me for skating with her. She was always so thoughtful and caring. She had a way of making me feel special, and I enjoyed spending a little bit of time with her. She was a connection to our family back home.

Skating was a good pastime at Marieval. I liked being on the ice, but I still had problems getting my skate laces tight enough so my ankles wouldn't be so wobbly. Occasionally, I would ask a supervisor to tighten my skate laces if he wasn't too busy, or I would also ask a senior boy to help me.

One day I overheard one of my friends asking a senior boy if he could tighten his laces. The senior boy said, "What will you give me if I tighten your laces?"

The junior boy promised him his lunch at four o'clock.

The supervisors never knew about this, and if they did know, they never said anything. But this practice continued throughout the winter months.

Sometimes when it snowed and we wanted to skate, we had to scrape the ice with snow scrapers and shovels that were kept in a shed next to the dressing room. Skating was fun for most boys, but for those who weren't that crazy about skating, there were always new shows like *The Flintstones*—an animated cartoon about two guys, Fred and Barney, who lived in the caveman era—coming on television.

It was fun watching them get into trouble and try to conceal things from their wives. Fred owned a small dinosaur who acted like he was a dog. His name was Dino.

He knocked Fred over and licked his face whenever he came home from work.

When it came to television programs, *Bonanza* was my favourite, and it came on at nine o'clock on Sunday evenings. It was about the adventures of the Cartwright family, who owned a large ranch called the Ponderosa. Thrice-widowed Ben Cartwright had three sons, each by a different wife. There were a few other TV shows I enjoyed like *The Texan* starring Rory Calhoun. He ran into a lot of outlaws, but his fast draw always managed to get him out of sticky situations.

In general, television was a source of entertainment, and it occupied a lot of our free time. Watching television helped us to forget about being stuck in this residential school. It became a fantasy world. Much like the books in our classrooms, it helped us to pass the time. We enwrapped ourselves in a television culture like so many other people were doing.

It had been quite some time since we last heard from Mom and Dad, so we asked Ernest to help us write a short letter to them. Hopefully, they were still working on that ranch in Alberta. This was the first time we had ever written a letter to anyone, so we weren't sure if Mom and Dad would receive it or not.

We wrote a short letter and did our best to copy the address down properly. We told Mom and Dad we were lonesome and we didn't like it here. But we also told them we were happy Dad was working in Alberta and getting to ride horses all the time. We thanked them for the money they sent because it came in handy for the bazaar. We signed off by telling them how much we loved them.

One day Father Carriere came down with some mail for us. When he called out Norman's name, I just knew it was a letter from our parents.

I could hardly wait to hear what Mom and Dad had to say. However, we were disappointed because the letter we wrote never reached them. It had *"Return to Sender"* stamped on it. When I looked at Norman for an explanation, it looked like he was going to cry. I tried to imagine why our letter would come back. Maybe we didn't write the address correctly on the envelope, or maybe Mom and Dad weren't working on that ranch anymore. It would have been nice for someone to help us write a letter so we could find out what was happening with our family.

One afternoon, I was playing outside when I noticed a senior boy walk towards the small boys' ball diamond, and he didn't stop. He walked into the bush by the ball diamond and kept on walking down toward the creek.

I wasn't going to tell anyone because he'd probably bust me up for ratting him out. His absence wasn't noticed until we were called into the playroom for supper.

That's when Mr. Dennis asked where he was and if anyone had seen him.

One of the boys said they last saw him going out to the playground and he was by himself.

Mr. Dennis asked all the boys who were out on the playground to raise their hands.

I raised my hand along with a few other boys.

He immediately summoned us to his office. "Okay, boys. What's going on?"

The other boys said they never noticed him out on the playground, so they were dismissed. Although I was the only one who saw him leave, my lips were sealed. It wasn't unusual for boys and girls to run away from Marieval, so when I was questioned further, I denied seeing him.

I don't remember that senior boy ever getting caught and returned to school. I think he was almost sixteen years old, so they probably just let him go.

Other times, boys were unsuccessful in running away. Their punishment was handed out in the form of a strap.

I wasn't a bad kid, but on occasion, I did get caught for trivial things like climbing on the pipes, coming in late when the whistle blew, losing one of my mitts, or whispering after the bell rang in the dining room.

I didn't do anything to warrant a strapping until this one time when I was playing outside. My friend, Randy and I were playing with his sling and competing with one another to see who could throw a stone the farthest.

He put a stone in his sling and sent it sailing past the football uprights.

I told him I could bounce a stone off the principal's roof.

He dared me to try it, so I loaded up a good-sized rock and let it fly. The only problem was, it fell a bit short of the roof and smashed his front picture window.

I told my friend, "Hey Pal, here's your sling," and I went racing into the playroom.

Shortly after, Mr. Dennis called everyone into the playroom and asked, "Who were the two boys playing near the football field?"

Randy and I looked at one another and raised our hands.

We were both taken up to the principal's office where Mr. Lang sat looking very serious.

He was angry and Father Carriere was seated beside him.

I was petrified, but I didn't want to get my friend, Randy into trouble. "I'm sorry. I hit the window by accident and I was using my sling."

They asked, "And what part did Randy play in all of this? Be honest and tell us who broke the window?"

I replied, "Randy was just watching me throw stones."

Father Carriere told Randy to go back to the playroom.

Then I stood there alone at the mercy of both principals. I guess you can say I was fortunate not to get strapped that day, but I did receive a stern lecture on how much money it was going to cost the school to replace that picture window. I also spent a lot of time kneeling in a corner to make up for what I did.

Back then I had a reputation as a good little boy, so when word got out, I had taken the blame for smashing Mr. Lang's picture window, it didn't sit well with the others.

Some of the boys told Randy I would never do something like that, so it must have been his fault. After all, I didn't even own a sling. They were ready to string him up until I told them it was my fault. However, I don't think they believed me.

After that incident, the boys labelled me as a solid kid for smashing the principal's window and owning up to it.

One morning, I glanced out our small boys' dormitory window and saw how much snow had fallen overnight. I was excited about playing outside and maybe even going sliding.

The mood in the playroom was good as we sat around waiting for the dining room bell to ring.

Mr. Gilbert informed us he would be putting a list of numbers on the bulletin board. "If your number is up there, you will be clearing snow off the sidewalks."

So many thoughts ran through my mind as we lined up for breakfast, but most of all, I could hardly wait to go outside and play in the snow.

When we were done eating, I checked the numbers on the bulletin board. My number wasn't on the list, so I went to the washroom where we kept our parkas and bundled up to go and play in the snow.

When I got outside, a fierce wind was blowing through the valley. It didn't take long for the cold to penetrate my parka, so I found shelter inside the dressing room where there was a warm stove going.

Ernest was in there rolling tape into a puck. He looked around for broken sticks and removed the tape from their blades. He took his time rolling the tape into the shape of a puck. Then, he showed me what it looked like when he was done. To my amazement, it didn't look too bad. At least now he had a puck.

We spent many hours in the dressing room, our refuge from the cold winds that howled outside. We talked about some of the hockey games the senior boys played against neighbouring towns last year and who the better players were on our side. We also talked about the junior boys' teams and how we looked forward to playing on a team against the girls.

Some of the boys recalled how much fun those games were and I could hardly wait to play against them. It sure sounded like a lot of fun.

My parents and younger siblings back home were always on my mind, especially during the lonely days at school.

I tried not to think about them, but life was so different here. Every day I wondered what was happening back home.

Our life there wasn't restricted with so many rules and we didn't have to pray all the time. Our diet was so much better and I couldn't remember being forced to eat something I didn't like. Mom's cooking was always delicious and most of our food came from the land or Grandpa's garden. Thinking about our life on White Bear made me homesick.

Norman wanted to go home too, and I pitied him when I saw him crying. There were times when he would go out on the playground just to be alone. When he came back inside, I could tell when he had been crying because his eyes were red. He looked sad and during those times he wanted to be left alone.

I tried to think of ways to cheer him up but there wasn't much I could do. Sometimes I could coax him into playing a game of Snakes and Ladders, checkers, or a board game called crokinole. In this game, players took turns shooting discs across a circular playing surface. They tried to have their discs land in the higher-scoring regions of the board while attempting to knock away opposing discs, much like in curling. This was a very popular game in our playroom.

Marieval observed many important dates. Remembrance Day was one of them. On Friday, November 11th, our teacher asked, "Who knows what special day this is?"

Ann raised her hand. "Yes, Ann what is today called?"

"It's called Remembrance Day."

"That's right. Many soldiers gave their lives so we can live a life of freedom. After recess, we'll be joining other students in the gymnasium to watch a film about some of the things that happened during the world wars. Pay attention to the film, so you will have a better understanding of what happened during the world wars and the Korean conflict."

When we arrived at the gym, some of the other students were already sitting there. The grade-one students had to sit in the front row while Sister Andre stood behind a projector and a record player.

She said, "Once I start the projector, you will watch the film in silence!"

On the screen, we saw pictures of soldiers marching off to war. Every so often I could hear the sound of a ding and Sister Andre would change the picture.

We watched a story of a soldier who told his friend he would take his place on a mission.

He said, "You have a wife and kids at home, but I don't have to worry about a family." It showed a picture of that soldier getting killed by a bomb.

The narrator said, "There's no greater love than giving your life for your country and your fellow man."

I thought about that film for a while and wondered, "Why do people have to go to war?"

At eleven o'clock, we stopped what we were doing, and Sister Andre said, "Let's observe a moment of silence to remember and honour all the soldiers who died in the two world wars and the Korean conflict. I hope we will never see another world war in our lifetime but we need to pray for all those who gave their lives for their country."

Later that day, there were all kinds of war shows on television. The shows we watched were about how mighty the Americans were and how they would always win the battles they fought.

I wanted to be a soldier when I grew up so I could help win another war. I thought of Sergeant Rock from my comics and how he was always fighting, but for some reason, he never got killed.

He got wounded a few times but that didn't hurt him. He put white bandages over his wounds and kept fighting until he won his battles.

I recalled seeing a picture of Dad in his military uniform.

He talked of the militia and sang military songs, but I don't think he ever went to war.

I had a cousin, James, who was in the Korean War and many other relatives who fought in World War II.

James was lucky to come home, but many more never returned home, like Grandpa Danny, and Grandpa Edward McArthur who we both killed in action.

World War 1 (1914-18) and World War II (1939-45) both saw a lot of casualties from our reserve. Dad told me a lot of our people died defending Canada even though they didn't have to go to war. It was a white man's war.

I think many students had relatives that went to war and never made it home. Someday, it might be our turn to fight in a war.

By the middle of November, we still hadn't heard from our parents, and we had no way of contacting them.

Some of the other boys were already talking about their plans for the Christmas holidays and how good it was going to be to get away from this place.

I kept hoping for a letter from Mom and Dad every time mail was distributed in our playroom. Were they on the reserve living next door to our grandparents?

One day, I asked Norman, "Can we write a letter to Grandma and Grandpa? They're always at home and might know why our parents aren't writing to us."

We asked Ernest, "Do you know our grandparents' mailing address?"

"No, but I'll ask one of the supervisors."

He went into their office and returned a short time later.

"Mr. Gilbert said put their names on the envelope, along with General Delivery, Carlyle, SK and the postmaster would put it into their mailbox. The letter should have a return address in the top left corner, but he'll help us fill out that section before he mails it for us."

Ernest said, "I'm not a very good speller but I'll help you sound out the words. Grandma likes getting mail and she'll probably be surprised to get a letter from us. She'll probably answer right away. I remember watching her sitting at the table and writing a letter to Auntie Mable when she moved to Carry-the-Kettle Nakoda reserve. She also wrote several letters to our other relatives in Regina."

Norman replied, "I never heard of them going anywhere during the winter because at times it's hard for them to find a driver. They go to town to shop and check their mail but most of the time they stay home."

So, we wrote a letter back home to our grandparents.

> *dear gramma*
>   *ware are our parenz livin? we hasn't herd frum dem fer a long tyme. If u see dem kin u tel dem to rite a lettr to us?*
>   *do u err see Ernests dad or hiz sistr faye arond? if u do how are dey dooin? kin u tel dem Ernests lonesum and he wuz asken how dey werr dooin. Iz enywun comin to git us for the crismass holidaz? if u do see mum and dad kin u tell dem to cum and git us for the holidaz? we doont wanna be stuk hare at sckool. we mis u and the rezt of da families. we are scared tht we mite be stuk hear at dis place and we are all very lonsum.*
> *Luv frum us.*

When we finished printing our letter, we gave it to Mr. Gilbert, who showed us how to put our return address on the envelope. We knew Grandma and Grandpa rarely went anywhere other than to Carlyle, so they should get our letter in a few days. We just had to wait for their reply.

Sure enough, Grandma eventually answered our letter. She wrote: Your dad is in jail for unpaid fines, and we aren't sure if we can find a driver to come and get you for Christmas. Your mom is in the Arcola hospital where she just gave birth to another baby boy. Tell Ernest his dad and Faye are both doing good.

Grandma signed off by telling us she hoped we were in the best of health and she loved us.

Now we understood why our parents weren't writing to us. That letter brought more uncertainty about our upcoming Christmas holidays.

I really hated this place and my longing to go home for Christmas was stronger than ever. I decided when I got a little older, I was going to run away from this place. I would run so far away no one would ever be able to find me.

One day near the end of November, our teacher informed us we were invited to be a part of the Christmas concert at the community hall. "Think of a song, a play, or a short skit you would like to perform at the concert."

Someone suggested we do a square dance like the one they do in *Country Hoedown* on TV.

Our teacher smiled and said it was a brilliant idea and we would have to start practicing soon.

Now I didn't know the first thing about square dancing, so I hoped I wouldn't have to dance at the concert.

Norman and Ernest got out of it, but somehow, my name ended up on the list.

We spent a lot of time practicing how to square dance.

Ms. Sedeski played music on a record player and gave us directions on how to square dance. It was awkward at first, but after a few sessions, I began to catch on to our routine.

I started to enjoy the music as I listened to the voice on the record player telling us what to do.

My square-dance partner was Sandra, and I learned how to dance with her. At the time, I needed more structure in my life and square dancing filled that void.

We were getting ready for our first concert. Just thinking about being in front of all those people made me nervous. Being in our classroom filled the lonely days and made life more bearable. However, the weekends were more of a challenge.

The weather played a large factor in what our schedule looked like. When it snowed too hard for us to skate, especially during blizzards, we were allowed to stay inside and watch TV.

Some of the boys who were bored with watching TV would go out to the dressing room or the gym where they could shoot baskets, or play floor hockey.

One day, I asked a supervisor, "Sir, will we be going sliding soon?"

"Well, it looks like there's enough snow on the hills. If things work out, we might go sliding on Saturday, but remember, it all depends on the weather."

I couldn't wait to tell Norman and Ernest the good news. I found them watching TV and said, "We might go sliding this weekend if the weather is good."

They both smiled. Ernest talked about some of the hills they had gone sliding down last year.

He said, "It's going to be so much fun! We should go sliding together."

I said, "I want to sit in the front of the toboggan."

He smiled and said, "Okay you can sit in the front."

I recalled the times we went sliding back home at our grandparents' place and how much fun we had.

That following Saturday, Mr. Gilbert said, "We're going sliding on a hill near the school. I'm going to open the shed where the toboggans and sleighs are stored. Some of you senior boys look after the junior boys and make sure they get a chance to slide."

Almost immediately, some of the senior boys pushed their way into the shed to get to their favourite ride. There was a mid-sized toboggan in there called *Snow-boy* that was legendary because it was light and sturdy. There was a mad scramble to grab that toboggan.

Ernest didn't get *Snow-Boy*, but he emerged with a large wooden toboggan that was roomy enough for the three of us.

There was quite a bit of snow on the hills, so when we got halfway up that first hill, Ernest said, "Okay I think this is high enough. Walter, sit in the front with your legs crossed. Norman, you can kneel behind him with your hands on his shoulders. You can use your feet to help steer the toboggan. I'm going to jump on after I give us a good push."

Everything sounded good, and before I knew it, we were flying down the hill and picking up speed. It was hard to see where we were going because of all the snow flying in my face. I was having difficulty breathing because we were going so fast! I didn't know whether to laugh or be scared. The ride down the hill was exhilarating, but it only lasted for a few minutes.

When we reached the bottom of the hill, I said, "Ernest I know why you wanted me to sit in the front. You wanted to hide behind me when we went through the snowbanks."

Ernest laughed. "You guys want to try it again?"

"Sure," I said. "But only if we stay on a packed trail."

The next ride down the hill was easier to handle because we didn't go as high up the hill as we had the first time, and we stayed on a path some of the other boys had already plowed through.

After a couple of enjoyable hours, we started to get cold because our pants and mitts were wet. We were glad to hear the whistle blow and it was time to head back to the school.

There was always something happening at Marieval. Sometimes a fistfight would break out, but we minded our business and never told on anyone. A few of the senior boys liked to pick on the younger ones. For me, it was a day scholar who came from a neighbouring reserve.

I don't know why he didn't like me, but every chance that came his way, he would look at me and call me an "ugly bugger." I quickly learned to avoid him but never told on him because there was no one to confide in other than John, and I didn't want to get him into trouble for fighting. If I told a supervisor, he would probably tell me to avoid him or quit being a sissy.

As a small boy, I saw a lot of lateral violence in that school. Violence was often found on the school grounds. Unless you had an older brother or friend for a backer, one of the school bullies would seek you out and ask for a fight.

One of my friends, Randy, was picked on a lot because they knew he wouldn't fight back. I often saw senior boys punching him in the arm until he cried. I watched a couple of boys hitting him and they kept on hitting him even though he was already crying.

Another person who was picked on quite often was Lum. He was a day scholar who never fought back, so he was an easy target for the bullies.

They watched for the supervisors, and when the coast was clear, they would punch him out.

He never told anyone about the physical abuse he was receiving because that would have made things worse.

I pitied Randy, Lum, and some of the other junior boys who were treated that way. The bullies were learning about violence from the nuns, priests, and staff who were constantly hitting the boys and girls with their knuckles, rulers, keys, and the strap.

While at Marieval, we were threatened with the strap for being bad. But on the other hand, they were teaching us how to be violent and hate one another.

One day, a fight broke out in the playroom that involved two senior boys. I could see them slugging it out. Both had blood coming from their mouths and noses. Nothing was done about it because I saw them in the dining room a short time later and I think they were ignored on purpose.

Other times, the supervisors turned a blind eye to fights on the ice or justified it as being a part of hockey. Fighting during a game wasn't corrected; instead, it became a penalty for five minutes and the game would go on.

I also watched fighting encouraged on *Hockey Night in Canada* with Foster Hewitt as the commentator. In particular, I remember Eddie Shack, who played hockey for the Toronto Maple Leafs.

He was famous for his fighting, rough play and entertainment. When he got into a fight on the ice, the boys would cheer for him.

I don't think I ever watched Eddie Shack play hockey without getting into a fight. Eventually, they made a song about him and the role he played as an enforcer and entertainer.

I often listened to the song's words: "Clear the track, here comes Shack, Eddie, Eddie Shack."

The supervisors didn't care if they saw someone crying. They either ignored them or yelled at them for being a sissy. There were rules for everything, and if the rules were broken in any way, someone had to pay for it. But, for some reason, fights were never completely stopped.

Many fights happened in the washroom or out on the playground. A time and a place to have it out could always be found if two boys wanted to get it on. Sometimes, if they got caught fighting, they would be sent to kneel or stand in the corner. For the more serious offences, the strap was used.

I overheard some of the senior boys talking about their visit to Mr. Lang's office where he kept a strap, with a wooden handle on it for a better grip.

The fear of going to hell was deeply ingrained into our daily lives, but any mention of our cultural traditions was seen as bad, evil, and the work of the devil. We spent a lot of time going to church because it was wrong to be an Indian, and the church was the only way to get to heaven.

Religion was at the heart of our teachings, while catechism classes helped prepare us for our First Communion. In some of these classes, we were taught about the book of Genesis and how God created Adam and Eve and put them in the Garden of Eden.

I thought about creation stories my grandfather shared with me as a child. They were different from what they were teaching us here.

At Marieval they taught us about the birth of Jesus and told us that's what Christmas was all about. It wasn't about receiving gifts but rather celebrating the birth of Jesus Christ. I couldn't understand why we were punished for saying his name. His name was considered swearing.

I listened with interest as our catechism teacher read us a story about Joseph and Mary going to Bethlehem and not being able to find a room to stay for the night. So, Jesus was born in a stable and placed in a manger.

As our teacher shared this story, it reminded me of the time when it was pouring rain outside. It was too wet to sleep in our tent, so my parents had me and my brothers sleep in our car. At the time, we were small enough to fit into the trunk where Mom made a bed for us.

Norman was lucky because he had the whole front seat to himself. Then Dad pulled the back seat down to make a bed for him and Mom to sleep on.

We weren't afraid of sleeping in the trunk because we could see Mom and Dad when the back seat was pulled down. We had no place to go, but at least we were warm and dry in the car just like baby Jesus in that stable.

The songs they were singing in the church were in celebration of Christmas too. They placed a Nativity scene up near the front where Jesus lay in a manger with some animals around him.

I couldn't recall my parents or grandparents celebrating Christmas back home on White Bear.

They never put up a tree with decorations, they didn't have a special dinner, and they didn't give one another gifts at Christmas.

Grandpa said, "We don't celebrate Christmas on one day of the year. We celebrate it year-round. We feed people who visit us and we give them gifts in giveaway ceremonies. We treat people special every day, and we share our good times with them. We love one another unconditionally, and that's what Christmas is all about."

Things were so different here. But somehow, I knew my family wasn't bad for celebrating Christmas every day of the year, not only on December 25th.

During class, I was starting to enjoy our square-dance routine for the Christmas concert which was quickly approaching. I was learning how to dance, but I was still shy of girls. When it came time to join hands with Sandra, my hands were sweating and I hoped she wouldn't notice.

She was a good dance partner. With each practice, I felt more confident and made fewer mistakes on the dance floor.

Ms. Sedeski said we were doing well, and she felt confident we would be ready for the concert on December 21st, which would be our last day of school.

Ernest said, "Most of the students go home for the holidays, but last year there were a few of us who stayed at school because we didn't have a ride home. It all depends on the road conditions. Sometimes the school arranges a ride home for the students."

I tried to stay positive and believe one way or another we were going home for the holidays. In the meantime, we would have to remain here and think positive.

There was a hockey schedule for the senior boys. We watched some games against Neudorf and Lebret.

The one against Neudorf was a very rough game with a lot of hitting and a couple of fights. Our team wore green jerseys and matching socks while Neudorf had red and white sweaters with mismatched socks.

This was one of the rare times the girls were allowed to come over to our side and cheer for the boys' team. The game was tied 3-3 going into the final period. It stayed that way until Neudorf scored a goal late in the period to go ahead, and that's how it ended.

The game against Lebret was not as physical, but there was a lot of passing and end-to-end rushes with both sides using their speed to make the game more exciting. In the end, the final score was Marieval 5 and Lebret 3.

The game ended around five o'clock, so the team was invited to stay and join us for supper. It was nice to see different boys sitting in the dining room. I knew the girls were excited too because they kept looking over to our side.

When we finished eating, it was time for our visitors to board their bus and head back to Lebret. The senior boys shook hands with them and wished them a safe trip home.

Music played a big part in our lives at school. A radio was always playing inside, but it also played on the playground through a loudspeaker. Country songs and some of the latest tunes from Chubby Checker and Elvis Presley could always be heard on the radio.

The senior boys and girls attended dances in the school gymnasium regularly, and I would occasionally see some of them practicing the twist in the playroom.

Music in the church took on a different theme as most of the songs were about the birth of Jesus; they sang songs like "Silent Night," "Away in A Manger," "O Come, All Ye Faithful," and "Joy to the World."

The day of our Christmas concert finally arrived and I was as nervous as a grasshopper in a hen house.

Our teacher told us we would be going over to the hall and the grade-one students would be sitting in the front rows.

We lined up and walked over to the hall in two rows just as she instructed us to do.

I walked beside Norman. When we arrived, we went straight to the front row. From this vantage point, we would be able to see the whole concert. These were the best seats in the house, but I was nervous about square dancing on stage. The hall was packed with students, staff members, and parents from Cowessess and neighbouring reserves along the valley. Excitement filled the hall.

Before the concert started, our teacher signalled for us to come to the stairs leading to the stage. We would be performing first, but we had to wait until the master of ceremonies introduced us.

The curtain to the stage was closed, but I heard Mr. Lang welcoming everyone to our Christmas concert. "To start the concert, the grade-one students will be performing a square dance under the guidance of their teacher, Ms. Sedeski."

When the curtain opened and I saw how many people there were in the audience, I got stage fright. The hall was packed with people, and some were still arriving. There were even spectators sitting in the balcony high above the crowd.

Our teacher assured us everything was going to be okay if we didn't look at the audience.

As the music started, I tried not to think of all the people watching us. During our dance routine, the girls were dancing in one spot while a boy went and bowed to one of them before taking her by the hand and promenading her around the dance floor.

When it was my turn, I bowed to the wrong dance partner. I could hear Ms. Sedeski, say "No, Walter."

After a moment, Sandra took my hand and we caught up to the other dancers.

At the end of our square dance, we lined up and bowed to the audience. I could hear them clapping in appreciation of our performance.

During the concert, some of the senior students played a piano or accordion, while others sang songs, recited poetry, or acted in a play.

When a choir sang "Here Comes Santa Claus," I heard a commotion at the back of the hall so I turned around to see what was happening.

Santa Claus was coming down the aisle! He was carrying a large white bag full of candies and small gifts. His face was red from the cold outside. What was going to happen next?

Then the announcer, Mr. Lang, told us to go up on stage and see what Santa Claus had for us.

He shook my hand. "Were you a good boy this year?"

I told him I had been a good boy. However, I forgot to tell him about breaking the picture window, hanging from the pipes, and not telling on the senior boy who ran away. But I thought he saw everything. If he did, he wouldn't have given me a candy cane, a Mandarin orange, and a mixed bag of candies and nuts.

Anyway, I thanked Santa Claus and went back to my seat.

As soon as Mr. Lang thanked everyone for coming to the concert, Ms. Sedeski told us to return to our classroom and pick up our report cards.

It was cold outside but the weather didn't look too bad.

I noticed there were quite a few cars parked near the hall so I knew the roads leading into the valley must have been good enough for the parents and spectators to make it to the concert. I quickly looked around the parking lot but didn't see our grandparents' car parked there.

Hopefully, Mom and Dad were on their way to pick us up for the holidays. It was going to be nice to go home and leave this hell hole behind.

Back in our classroom, our teacher congratulated us for dancing so well at the concert. She never said anything about my mistake on stage so maybe no one even noticed it. Instead, she told us how proud she was of our performance.

When she handed out our report cards, I noticed the name on my report card said, Walter Grant and not Robert Gary like I hoped it would.

As I quickly glanced at my marks, I was happy to see they were all good even the ones in art and arithmetic.

Ms. Sedeski said she was happy with our first term and if we continued to work hard, we would all pass our grades.

She permitted us to take our artwork down from the windows and place it in our scrapbooks so we could take it home and show it to our families. She wished us a Merry Christmas and said she would be seeing us after the holidays. Then she dismissed us from class.

We returned to our playroom while the day scholars boarded their buses. A few of the boarders were lucky enough to be leaving the school with their parents. There were also a few students who lived within walking distance from the school and they left as soon as we were dismissed.

I sat quietly with Norman and Ernest, wondering if we were going home for the holidays or if we would be staying here. It was amazing to see how quickly our playroom emptied and before long there were only a few of us left.

Mr. Gilbert said he was going to turn on the television because he didn't want anyone going outside in case our parents came to the school to pick us up. He reminded us he would be in the supervisors' office and he did not want anyone to leave without letting him know. It was still early and some of our parents could be on their way to pick us up.

When Mr. Gilbert went into his office, I joined Norman who was sitting on a chair near the front of the TV.

I noticed he wasn't watching the television but he was looking out an iced-up window.

He was quiet but I could hear him sniffling and trying his best not to cry. When he looked at me, I could see tears welling up in his eyes. He looked sad and although he didn't say anything, I could tell he was lonesome and didn't think we were going home for Christmas.

I didn't know what to say to him without making him cry, so I sat beside him hoping my companionship would make him feel better. I crossed my fingers and listened for the sound of footsteps coming down the stairs and someone informing us our parents were in the parlour waiting to take us home. But it never happened.

As I sat beside Norman in the playroom, I asked him, "Are you going to take your scrapbook home to show your artwork to Mom and Dad?"

"Yeah, I have a couple of pictures I want to show them. What about you?"

"No, I don't have any pictures to show them. I'm just going to take my report card home."

"Well, what did you do with your scrapbook?"

"I left it at my desk so Mom and Dad wouldn't laugh at my funny pictures. Maybe next time I will have some better ones to show them."

I was happy when Ernest came and joined us.

He smiled and asked us what we were talking about?

Norman told him we were talking about what we were going to take home to show our parents. He asked Ernest what he was taking home?

Ernest replied, "I'm going to take home a couple of my drawings, my report card and a couple of Western comic books for Grandpa."

I said, "I forgot he likes to read those comics. Sometimes he uses a magnifying glass to read them. I should have saved him a comic like *The Rawhide Kid*, or *Kid Colt Outlaw*. I'll have to remember it the next time we go home for the holidays. That will be a nice surprise for Grandpa."

Ernest asked if we thought our dad was out of jail for his unpaid fines? He said he was a bit worried our grandparents wouldn't have a driver to come for us. If that was the case we might be stuck here for the holidays.

Norman said he recalled Uncle Willie going to jail for unpaid fines and he was out in a few weeks. If Dad was at home, he was sure Mom would send him for us.

"I don't want to miss our grandparents' feast because the food here can't compare to the food, they serve on New Year's Day. Everything at the feast tastes so yummy."

Ernest said, his dad liked to hunt for the feast and he wanted to go with him when he went hunting in the park. He went on to say, Uncle Ernie, let him shoot ducks, but he wanted to learn how to track and hunt deer too.

Norman said he liked to set snares for Grandma and Mom but he also liked the idea of learning how to shoot a rifle. He recalled watching Dad shoot at a deer and it didn't look that hard to use a rifle. But a shotgun now that was too scary.

I said I wanted to go hunting with them too because I was a good shot with a bow and arrow.

They both laughed and Norman said I could tag along with them and bring my bow and arrow.

He said if I killed a moose Mom and Dad would be so proud of me because we would have enough meat to last us for a long time.

I could hear Ernest chuckling and I knew they were making fun of me. I quickly looked at Norman who was winking at Ernest so I knew they were teasing me.

As we talked, we heard footsteps coming down the stairs and held our breath. We looked at one another and hoped we were going home for the holidays.

Chapter 5 - Christmas Holidays at Home

I couldn't believe it when Father Carriere came down the stairs and called our names. "Ernest, Norman, and Walter! Grab your things and come with me to the parlour. There's someone here to see you." I was so excited! Mom and Dad were standing in the parlour smiling!

Dad said, "Ernest, your grandparents couldn't make it, but they want you and Shirley to come home with us."

On the way home, we told Mom Ms. Sedeski gave us our report cards. She read Norman's report card. "Norman, you're doing well in school," she told him and smiled.

Then she read my report card. "Gary, you have the wrong report card! This one belongs to Walter Grant, not you. Your teacher must have given you the wrong report card."

"I know, Mom. Our teacher started calling me Walter during the first day of class, and that's what everyone calls me now. I tried to tell her my name wasn't Walter but she said in her class I would answer to the name of Walter Grant"

Mom said, "Well when you get back to school tell them your name is Robert Gary, not Walter Grant." She didn't understand how much I tried to convince my teacher she was calling me the wrong name.

When we arrived home on White Bear, it was nice to see Grandma and Grandpa again. Our little brother, Oranges, grinned at us and took off into the bedroom when we smiled at him. We could hear him talking, "Mom how long are they going to be at home with us?"

"They'll be home until their Christmas holidays are over, about ten days. Then they have to return to school."

After we put away our coats, boots, and mitts, Mom called us into the bedroom and unrolled some blankets to show us the newest addition to our family, a little boy.

"What's his name?" I asked.

"Frederick." Then she looked worried as she told us there was something wrong with his right leg. "He was born with polio, and when he gets older, he will always walk with a limp. There is nothing they can do for him because there is no cure for polio."

I felt sorry for my little brother because I couldn't imagine what it would be like for him to grow up not being able to walk normally like other kids. Then I remembered a couple of boys at school who had polio and both of them walked with a limp.

The other boys never teased them, but I could tell the senior boy felt self-conscious when the girls stared at him.

I hoped my little brother wouldn't feel the same way.

After talking with Mom for a while I went into the other room to sit and chat with our grandparents. I told them about how mean the nuns, priests, and supervisors were at school. I shared our experience of waking up one Sunday morning thinking we were coming home, but instead, we went to church. "Grandma, I love being at home. Everything here is so natural and cozy. I missed the smell of the wood smoke and the crackle of the fire in the woodstove and heater. And guess what? We almost caught a rabbit when we went for a walk, but it got away."

Norman looked so much happier now that we were home. He asked, "Grandma, do you have any snare wire? I want to set some snares in the morning."

"I'll go look for it. I know I put some away recently."

She found it a short while later, so we sat around the table cutting the wire and putting loops in them. Now, all we had to do in the morning was place the snares over rabbit trails.

We asked Mom, "Have you guys eaten any rabbit stew this winter?"

That's when she told us Uncle Victor and Auntie Edna were living next door in the old log shack with their seven children. That was exciting to hear because it meant we were going to have a lot of company for setting snares and sliding down the hills.

Grandma said, "Tomorrow, I am going to stop in at Cochrane's Hardware Store in Carlyle to buy more snare wire in case we run out."

As she spoke, she looked at Grandpa. "Remind me to buy more saw blades from the hardware store because you only have one left."

Early the next morning Grandpa's shuffling footsteps in the kitchen woke me up. There was no mistaking the sound his moccasins made on the linoleum floor. I listened as he put wood in the heater and started a fire in the woodstove so Mom could cook breakfast for us.

Mom said, "He gets up every few hours during the winter nights to keep the fire going so we won't get cold. It doesn't take long for the house to get cold if the fire dies out."

I could hear Mom and Grandma talking in the kitchen. So, I wasn't dreaming. We were home for the holidays!

I could hardly wait to taste Mom's home-cooked meals. I wanted to set rabbit snares and go sliding. I also looked forward to exploring some of the trails around our home, especially the one that went by the clothesline and led to a place we called *"the hollow."* Maybe that would be a good place to set rabbit snares.

After a hearty breakfast, we dressed to go and catch rabbits. Oranges saw us putting on our boots, so he asked Mom if he could tag along with us.

She thought it would be nice for him to get fresh air. "Make sure and look after him and wait for him when you walk through the deep snow. You should also go next door to let them know you are home for the holidays. I'm sure they'll be glad to see you."

When we were outside, we saw smoke coming from the stovepipe next door, so we knew they were awake. We knocked on their door and heard someone approaching.

Uncle Victor answered the door and smiled when he saw us. "Hi! Come inside and visit for a while"

Our cousin, Shorty asked what we were going to do.

"We're on our way to the bush to set rabbit snares."

"Wait for me. We can go and check my snares. I set five of them just west of here. There are a lot of rabbits this year."

Auntie Edna said, "There are a lot of mouths to feed in our extended family, so it's a good thing you're going to set more snares. Is your grandma going to town today? If she is, I'd like to catch a ride to town to buy groceries."

Norman said, "I'm pretty sure she is. She talked about buying snare wire and saw blades from the hardware store.

She'll probably come over here to ask if you need anything from town."

"You're right. She comes over before she goes to town."

When Shorty was ready, our other cousins Klyne, Ross, and Tattums decided they wanted to come along too.

We were wondering what to do because there were eight of us and then Farren showed up. That's when Uncle Victor told Tattums to take the younger ones sliding while the rest of us went to the bush. Everyone was happy with that idea.

Shorty handed me a gunny sack. "Come up west with me to check my snares."

Ernest and Norman wanted to go down *the hollow* to look for rabbit trails. There was a lot of snow this winter so they hoped there would be some good trails past the clothesline.

On our way to the bush, Shorty and I walked on some tracks made by a team of horses pulling a sleigh. Shorty said Uncle Gordon passed by here quite often on his way to get a load of wood. People bought firewood from him so that kept him busy. He thought it would be better to follow the sleigh tracks so we wouldn't have to walk through the deep snow.

We caught a lot of rabbits as we checked Shorty's snares and the gunny sack was starting to get heavy.

Shorty said, "You're my good luck charm. I've never caught so many rabbits before."

A couple of them were still alive. I pitied one that was squealing and kicking to get away, but it didn't take long for Shorty to end his suffering.

When we got back from the bush, Uncle Victor was surprised to see how many rabbits there were in the gunny sack. "Shorty, leave them inside the porch. I'll get Doreen and Marie to skin them later. You can go and see how Norman and Ernest are doing in the bush."

We didn't have to go far because they got back to the house just as we were leaving to go and look for them.

They had huge smiles on their faces.

Norman said they found three good rabbit trails on their way to the well so they set three snares there. Then they went down *the hollow* and found three more bunny trails at the bottom. The snow was deep in that area and there were no signs anyone had been there for a while.

Ernest said, "That was a good place to set our snares because there was no human scent to scare the rabbits away."

After carefully setting their snares along three well-used trails, they decided to come back to the house to warm up.

Our grandparents' car was gone from its usual parking spot, so we figured they must have gone to town while we were in the bush. But it looked like the younger ones were having fun sliding on the hill beside our grandparents' place.

After we warmed up and had a quick lunch, we went back outside to haul in more wood for the stove and heater. We filled the firewood box and emptied the slop pail.

We spent the rest of the afternoon sliding on a hill behind the house. It was a steeper terrain than the hill in front of the house and we picked up more speed sliding on that hill.

After we went down a few times and packed a trail, we could fly down that hill and the ride was exhilarating. We were all laughing when we slid to the slough and stopped on the ice. It took us a while to get back to the top, but the ride down was well worth the climb. We tired the younger ones out, so we brought them back to the house.

Later that afternoon we went to check our snares again to see if we caught anything.

Norman and Ernest were lucky at setting snares because they caught two rabbits, but one of them was still alive.

Ernest looked around for a stick to hit it on the head with.

Norman laughed as he held the rabbit in the air and the snare wire tightened around its neck. It choked on the wire. He told Ernest, "You have to let it kick until it pees. Then you know it's dead."

When they brought the rabbits home Shirley told them to put them on top of the firewood box and she would help Mom skin and cook them later.

It was nice to see our grandparents' car get back from town just as it was getting dark. We helped them haul in the groceries while Shorty and Klyne helped their mom haul in her groceries for next door.

Mom asked Shorty, "Did you check your snares?"

He replied, "Klyne helped me, but we didn't catch anything. Hopefully, we'll catch something in the morning"

Mom laughed. "You must have played Oranges out because Shirley said he fell asleep as soon as he came inside. He was out as soon as his little head hit the pillow. When she checked on him later, he was snoring with his little mouth wide open."

For supper, Mom cooked neckbones she bought in town and they tasted so good. It had been a long time since we ate neckbones. Mom looked happy when we told her how much we missed her cooking.

We were enjoying our supper when Oranges came into the kitchen with his messy hair and a sleepy look on his face. You could tell he had a good nap, and he hid his face when Grandpa said, "Oh, look! The moon is up."

After we finished eating, we sat quietly waiting for Grandpa to refill his cup with tea.

Then he pushed his chair back and said, "By golly, you know one time."

His storytelling began and we sat there quietly listening for his story to unfold. We didn't have a television set, so Grandpa's stories were our source of entertainment.

That night, he talked about some farmers who tried to move a grain elevator in Carlyle. They hooked up several teams of draft horses to the elevator. Some of the horses stood as tall as 18 hands high and weighed 2,000 pounds but the elevator was too heavy for them to move.

One of the men said his friend had a team of oxen that could move the elevator.

The rest of the farmers laughed at him. So, he told them he would go ask his friend to come and move the elevator for them and they laughed even harder.

They waited patiently while he went to get his friend and his team of oxen.

When he returned, they watched as the team of oxen was hooked up to the elevator. Slowly the oxen strained against their yokes and the farmers could hardly believe their eyes when the elevator slowly started to move.

The farmer with the team of oxen smiled at the men and asked them where they wanted their elevator?

Grandpa said, "Them oxen moved the elevator that day and no one laughed after that." It was nice to be home listening to Grandpa's stories again.

I woke up early the next morning to the smell of bacon frying. I sat up and looked around in disbelief. I wasn't dreaming. We were at home.

When I got up to wash my face and hands, Mom asked, "How did you sleep?"

I smiled, "Mom I slept great. It's nice to be home again."

After a wholesome breakfast, we took Oranges with us to check our snares again. This time, we caught two rabbits and a prairie chicken.

When we took our catch back to the house, Mom said, "Before you do anything else, I would like you to bring in some snow to melt for water."

Then, we hauled in wood and filled the firewood box. We cut some kindling for starting a fire in the morning and Mom reminded us to empty the slop pail and bring it back inside.

When it looked like we were finished doing chores, she asked us to bring in the clothes from the line. We all pitched in to help, and it didn't take long to bring the clothes inside.

They didn't use a washing machine during the winter.

Mom washed the clothes by hand using a washtub and a scrub board. Then she hung them outside on the clothesline.

After we finished doing our chores, we asked if we could use the toboggan to slide down the hill near the house. We wanted to go sliding before exploring some of our old hangouts. This time we let Oranges sit in the front, but he didn't mind it because the hill wasn't as steep as the one, we were sliding on yesterday. Furthermore, the snow was already packed down from the sleighs and teams of horses going by.

We played on that hill until Mom reminded us to check our snares. It felt good to be at home for the holidays, and I thought about Grandpa's teachings about Christmas.

On Christmas Eve, some of the adults like our aunties and older cousins went to Midnight Mass, which was held at the Catholic Church not far from our place.

Everyone at our grandparents' place was more excited about our annual New Year's Day feast than they were about Christmas. This was our time of celebration, and from as far back as I could remember, our grandparents celebrated New Year's Day with a feast that was open to everyone. Friends and relatives came from all over the reserve to visit with us.

Our family spent a whole year preparing for this special occasion. For feast food, there were all kinds of wild meat, soups, and assorted vegetables such as sweet pickles, dill pickles, radishes, cucumbers, canned beets, turnips, carrots, cranberries, salads, and potatoes with gravy. Grandpa always made sure there was no ham or pork served during the feast because it was not considered to be a traditional food.

Grandma used her special cups and dishes for this momentous occasion, and everyone was encouraged to have second helpings. For dessert, there was usually jello, raisin sauce, puddings, pies, cakes, canned saskatoons, raspberries or strawberries, and rhubarb.

Mom and our extended family kept setting the table over and over again, feeding all the visitors who came to the feast.

Our visitors went to other homes that were hosting similar feasts so their whole day was spent visiting different families where they socialized and ate.

The older family members in our home visited and feasted with our guests until nine o'clock. Usually, the last person to come was Uncle Gordon, who came driving a sleigh pulled by a team of horses.

Mom asked me about the things I was learning at school.

I told her about catechism lessons, the church, and the Christmas concert. "Mom, why is it wrong to be an Indian? And why don't we pray every day as we do at Marieval?"

"Would you feel better if I dressed up like a nun and your dad dressed up like a priest?"

I tried to imagine them dressed like that and laughed. "You would look funny." I told her, "No, I don't think that would be right because the nuns and priests do things differently. They dress and act spooky"

She smiled because she knew I understood it was not wrong to be an Indian.

They just didn't understand us; they didn't even know my real name. It felt good to be at home with our parents while it lasted. Although there were chores to do around the house, the majority of our time was spent sliding or exploring the great outdoors.

Our grandparents had two dogs, Snap and Molly. Snap was a very friendly black reserve mutt, while Molly was a black-and-white dog with big floppy ears. Both of them liked home-cooked meals because it was their job to wolf down leftovers from the dinner table, including Grandma's leftover porridge. The dogs followed us when we went to check our snares, and sometimes, we chased them home because they ran ahead of us and scared the rabbits away.

One day I went next door with Shirley to the log shack where our cousins were living. She wanted to visit Doreen, Marie, and Tattums, who were eager to talk to us about going to school at Marieval.

Marie asked us, "What is it like going to school there?"

Shirley told her, "The nuns and supervisors are strict and mean. I'm not allowed to talk to Ernest or any of my male cousins, so you won't be able to talk to your brothers either. The nights in the dorm are lonely. I can hear the junior girls crying, but there is nothing I can do to help them. The girls are physically abused or threatened with the strap. I even heard stories about rape and sexual abuse from some of the senior girls. You will have to get used to praying from the time you get up until the time you go to bed." She looked into their eyes. "I don't want to go back there, but I don't have a choice. If possible, go to another school because you won't like it at Marieval."

While we were home, we enjoyed each day to the fullest. We woke up with a smile and went to bed with a smile. It was nice to be away from Marieval, but we also knew our holidays would soon be coming to an end.

On Saturday, January 7th, 1961, Mom woke us up early so we could get ready for our long ride back to the school.

We went next door to say farewell to our extended family.

They told us how much they enjoyed our company during the Christmas holidays.

Uncle Victor said, "Your cousins might be joining you soon at Marieval because my application for a new house on the Kahkewistahaw reserve has been approved. Show them the ropes if they start school there. Did you know that Kahkewistahaw means "Eagle flying in the air?"

Shirley smiled, "That's very interesting but I don't speak Saulteaux or Cree. I'm an Assiniboine remember? Uncle Norman would know what it means. He speaks Cree."

Shorty told me, "Tattums will be in the same grade as you, but I will be one grade higher while Marie and Doreen will be in grades seven and eight. Alvina, and Ross, will be in the lower grades, so they will be stuck in that residential school the longest. I'm looking forward to a bigger house on Dad's reserve, but I'm not happy about going to school at Marieval as a boarder."

Before leaving home, we hugged our younger siblings and told them how much we loved them and we would see them in the spring when we came home again for our next holidays. We told our grandparents we had a lot of fun during our holidays and thanked them for making sure we made it home.

Grandma hugged us and said, "It was nice to have you home for a while. I wish your holidays were longer. Thank you for setting snares and bringing home the rabbits for us. Don't worry about us while you're gone because Shorty and Klyne always drop off rabbits for us all the time."

This was a sad time for us. We were quiet on our way back to the school, but we did convince Mom and Dad to stop at Mr. Leost's convenience store near the school.

"Can we buy some candies to take to school with us?"

When we walked into the store, Mr. Leost smiled when he saw Dad. You could tell he remembered him and was happy to see him. He looked at me and Norman. "I just received a new shipment of comics this morning and you are my first customers."

We looked around the store and bought junk food like chips, pop, and jawbreakers.

Norman asked Mom, "Can I buy a tube of Brylcreem?"

To my surprise, she bought it for him, and he put some in his hair right away.

When we finished shopping at the store, Mom and Dad gave us a ride to the school and walked us to the parlour.

Before leaving, Mom told us they would come and visit us soon. They hugged us and we cried because we knew we wouldn't be seeing them again for a long time.

It was hard to imagine why we were here to learn about a different way of life when there was nothing wrong with being an Indian. The nuns, priests and staff at Marieval were constantly telling us, "Thou Shalt Not Be an Indian."

I didn't know how I could ever stop being an Indian to satisfy them. That is something I would have to work on if I wanted to go to heaven. I certainly didn't want to go to hell as my ancestors did!

Chapter 6 - A Cruel Winter

Father Carriere brought us back to the playroom and told a supervisor we were back from our holidays. I was surprised to see how many students had not returned yet. The playroom looked empty and I envied the day scholars and the boys who were at home enjoying their holidays. It would have been nice to spend one more night with our family.

Mr. Dennis said, "You boys still have enough time to go skating or you can stay inside to watch TV. I unlocked the dressing room so I know there are a couple of boys out there. I'll blow my whistle when it is time to come in and get ready for supper."

"Norman, what do you want to do? Do you want to go skating or do you want to stay in and watch TV?"

He looked at me then shrugged his shoulders and said, "I'll probably stay inside to see what's on TV. You can go skating if you want. Ask Ernest to see what he wants to do"

I decided to stay inside too. We didn't have a television set at home and I missed watching it.

We were in for a pleasant surprise; Mr. Dennis told us we were going to the gymnasium at eight o'clock that evening to watch a movie called *Jessie James*.

After supper, Mr. Dennis came into the playroom with a big grey blanket and opened it in the centre of the room, revealing several shorts of various colours and sizes. "Pick out a pair of shorts that will fit you and jump in the showers. One of us supervisors will be joining you shortly."

Without thinking too much about it, I grabbed a large brown pair of shorts and followed the other boys into the shower. When my shorts got wet, they became heavy and I had to hold on to them with one hand so they wouldn't fall.

Before I realized what was happening, a supervisor grabbed me and started to rub me down with a bar of soap, even beneath my shorts.

I was trying to hold up my shorts with one hand while trying to keep the soap out of my eyes with the other hand. That was the worst feeling in the world. It seemed like forever before he let me go.

I raced out of there because I didn't like the thought of someone touching my private parts. I wanted to tell Norman how I felt about it, but it was too embarrassing. I wished Mom was around so I could tell her.

She always had a good answer for everything and would tell me what to do.

At eight o'clock that evening we went to the gym only to find the girls were already sitting there. They sat on one side of the gym and the boys sat on the other side. There was a small aisle between the boys' and girls' sections, and I could see them passing treats to one another. I pulled out some snacks Mom bought for us earlier at Mr. Leost's store.

A few senior boys bought pop from a machine near the stairs, so I joined them and bought myself a ginger ale.

When the movie started, my eyes were glued to the screen because I loved Western movies. It was about Jesse James, his older brother, Frank, and their gang of outlaws. In the movie, the gang held up banks, stagecoaches, and trains.

A supervisor told us, "Much of this movie is fictitious, but some parts are based on true events. In the wild west, there was a James gang who became famous for their robberies."

I felt sorry for Jesse James when one of his gang members shot him in the back as he was hanging a picture on a wall.

A narrator said, Robert Newton Ford was best known for killing his gang leader Jesse James in April 1882. He wanted to collect a reward and an amnesty for past crimes.

I certainly would not be proud of shooting someone in the back, but Robert Ford and his brother Charles were paid for re-enactments of the killing at publicity events. I instantly disliked Robert Ford and his older brother Charles.

When the show ended, I knew it was time for bed because at school we usually went to bed by eight o'clock and it was past that time.

As we headed up the stairs to our dorm, I wondered if Grandma Smoker would be sitting in her usual chair waiting for us. I was disappointed when Sister David was there instead of Grandma Smoker.

She told me I would be moving to the other room because one of the junior boys had problems and needed to be closer to the washroom.

I knew what she meant, so I didn't ask any questions. I was happy to be sleeping in the same room as Norman and Ernest and I wasn't considered a little boy anymore.

She told us to change into our pyjamas and brush our teeth because she was going to turn out the lights as soon as we said our prayers.

I wondered where Grandma Smoker was and if she was coming back to the school.

Some of the small boys were crying in the dark so I sat up in bed, wondering if Norman was crying. Before I knew it, Sister David was standing next to my bed and telling me to go to sleep. She floated around like a ghost, so it was difficult to hear her coming and going.

On Sunday morning, we were up early to go to church. The nativity scene and animals had been removed from the front of the church, and the congregation no longer sang Christmas carols. We didn't have catechism classes because many of the students had not returned from their holidays.

I had a difficult time keeping my eyes open during Father Carriere's long sermon. My head bobbed around as I tried my best to stay awake. I kept thinking of Mom and Dad wondering if Dad set any more rabbit snares. Had he gone to the good places I told him about to look for trails in the bush?

I also found myself thinking about the time we went with Dad to check his muskrat traps during the holidays. I used to see those little brown huts on the sloughs, but I never knew what they were. I discovered the little huts were homes for the muskrats much like the beaver had homes on the ice.

After what seemed like an eternity, the sermon was over. I was relieved when they served Communion, which meant the service was almost over.

Our procession back to the school was so much smaller this morning and during breakfast, the dining room was half empty. We talked about our favourite memories of the holidays, including the movie we saw last night. It felt strange being back at Marieval.

"Ernest, how long will it be before we go home again for the holidays? I hate this place."

"We won't be going home until Easter," he said.

Not sure when that would be, I asked, "When is Easter?"

"Easter is in the spring or the beginning of April," he said.

My heart sank. That was three months away! Three more months trapped here! I felt like crying.

Laughter came from the supervisors' dining room. How could they be so happy in this place when there was so much misery for us?

I didn't feel like skating that afternoon, but I went to the dressing room with Norman while he strapped on his skates for a game of shinny. I stood along the boards watching him as he practiced raising a puck against the boards.

He coaxed me into putting on my skates and joining him.

I didn't feel like playing, but at least it was something to do. When Norman let me have a try at raising the puck, I surprised myself by getting it a couple of feet off the ice.

We kept practicing until there were about six of us on the ice then we decided to have a game of shinny. Since there were only a few of us, I had a chance to play forward. That was so much more fun than being stuck in the net.

Ernest watched me shoot the puck. "Why do you shoot the puck with your left hand when you're right-handed?"

"What do you mean?" I asked.

He showed me how he shot the puck on his right. He said, "Whenever you play hockey, look for a left-handed stick." He taught me how to tell the difference between a right-handed stick and a left-handed one.

I learned something new that afternoon and tried to shoot the puck with my right hand, but it felt awkward, so I kept shooting on my left.

Later in the day, more students arrived at the school. They were told to take a shower while the rest of us watched *The Ed Sullivan Show*.

When they were done taking their showers, I heard a couple of the junior boys crying in the playroom. I wanted to talk to them. But before I could do that, Mr. Dennis told them to come and sit down because he wanted to turn off the lights so the rest of us could watch *Bonanza*.

Norman and I joined some of the boys who pulled out chips, pop, and snacks while they watched the show.

As usual, everyone was silent when it started. It felt good to hear that familiar music in the beginning when Ben Cartwright and his sons rode up to the front of the set.

We didn't know what tonight's show was about because we missed the last episode where they showed a preview.

Most of the junior boys sat cross-legged on the floor, but I noticed a couple of them laying down while they used their friends' legs for pillows. I thought this was neat, but I preferred to sit up as it was easier to use the washroom during commercials.

When *Bonanza* was over, Mr. Gilbert turned off the television set. "Line up for bed now."

In the junior boys' dorm, Sister David gave us a small scoop of powder to brush our teeth.

When we finished in the washroom, she told us to put on our pyjamas and kneel beside our beds. Then she had us pray with her before turning out the lights.

I could hear a lonely boy crying in the dark. I lay there and wondered what everyone was doing back home. I could feel tears welling up in my eyes, so I covered my head with my pillow and had a good cry.

Why did we have to be here when there were two schools on the reserve and another one in Carlyle? Why did some students attend school on White Bear where they could go home every afternoon? We were so far away yet we learned the same things we could learn at home.

It didn't make sense and I couldn't figure it out. At least if I went to school back home, people would call me by my proper name. That night, I fell asleep thinking about Mom and Dad.

The next morning, I woke up when Grandma Smoker turned on the lights. I was surprised to see her in the dorm.

She must have arrived sometime during the night. She was a quiet lady of very few words, but when she pointed to the washroom with her lips, we knew what she meant.

We were taught at a young age not to use our fingers to point. Not only was it disrespectful but pointing with our fingers could be seen as a challenge by certain spirits. To be on the safe side we were taught to use our lips to point.

We lined up, waiting for our turn to use the washroom so we could wash up for breakfast. When everyone was ready, we stood by the exit door, waiting for a supervisor to come and get us.

Sister David appeared out of nowhere. She came up the steps without making a sound. How could she walk so quietly with her leather shoes? "Follow me," she said then escorted us downstairs to our playroom.

When we got there, Mr. Gilbert said, "Have a seat on the benches according to your numbers." He reminded us of our schedule for the day then told a couple of the senior boys they would be flooding the ice after class. The numbers for the snow brigade were also called out. The rest of us were told to stay off the ice and out of the way of the ones clearing the sidewalks.

As we lined up for breakfast, Mr. Gilbert went up and down the rows handing out little black vitamin C pills. "These pills are vitamin sunshine. Be careful not to bite them because they are bitter. You will be getting one each morning before breakfast."

When you tell someone not to do something, they're bound to do it. I watched Puchees bite his pill. It was dark orange on the inside and he said it tasted good. I tried it and discovered how bitter and horrible it tasted.

He laughed at me for being silly enough to listen to him.

I promised myself not to listen to him anymore and I could hardly wait to get into the dining room to wash that pill down with milk.

Mr. Gilbert saw me making a bitter face. "If you prefer, you do have the option of taking cod liver oil. Some of you know what that tastes like."

I couldn't answer, so I shook my head no. I remembered taking that stuff at home. It tasted horrible, and the juice Mom gave us to wash it down didn't make it taste any better.

Before saying grace, Sister Superior welcomed us back and gave us a long talk about the rules of the dining room. She went on to say, "Soon, we're going to be switching from plates to trays. Everyone will be responsible for getting their food from a cafeteria line. This means there will be very little table service in the dining room. However, this won't apply to the staffs' dining room."

Many of us must have looked confused, so she explained it a little more. "Upon entering the dining hall, you will form a line and pick up trays that are specifically designed to hold different food items. Then you will walk by a line of servers who will fill your trays with food. Remember, you are to eat all the food you're given whether you like it or not."

Some of the senior boys said they had seen this system before in hospitals and schools they attended.

I guess Marieval was a little behind the times.

During breakfast, I recalled Sister Andre's advice to put peanut butter and syrup on our toast. It was a good way to end our breakfast, but it sure made my orange taste sour. In the future, I would eat my fruit before eating syrup or honey.

After dismissal when we were back in our playroom, Mr. Dennis said, "Look at the bulletin board and check out the new hockey schedule I just posted."

When I read the bulletin board, I was surprised. What caught my eye was a list of the junior boys who would be playing a game of hockey on Saturday afternoon against the senior girls. Wow! This should be fun! Although I couldn't skate very well, I could play goal wearing my winter boots instead of skates. But as I looked at the list, my name or number wasn't on there. I saw Ernest's, Norman's, and Richard's names on the board, but no matter how many times I read it, I couldn't find my number. So, I asked Mr. Dennis why my name wasn't on the list to play on Saturday.

He said, "There are too many junior boys to put everyone on the team. Don't worry. There will be more games against the girls, and you'll get a chance to play."

I knew he was right, but it didn't make me feel any better.

During the week, I kept thinking about the hockey game against the girls and how much fun it was going to be to watch them play. I found myself wishing I was a better skater like Ernest so I could play in the game and maybe even score a goal for our team.

Sometimes when I played goal during a game of shinny my feet would get cold, so I hoped the weather on Saturday would be warm, especially for the spectators. However, it's difficult to predict the weather.

As the weekend rolled around, it was 15 degrees below zero. It was a bit chilly, but still, the game would go on as scheduled.

Inside the dressing room, Mr. Gilbert read out the starting line-up for the junior boys' team. He called out the names of some of our best players.

My friend, Steve, was going to be our captain.

I watched him as he made the letter "C" out of hockey tape and put it on his left shoulder.

Shickle was the alternate captain, so he taped the letter "A" on his sweater in a similar fashion.

During the first period, the girls came into our end three or four times, but they never scored. There was a lot of action at the other end as the boys scored time and time again.

By the end of the first period, we were ahead 5-0. Instead of taking an intermission, the referee told the teams to switch ends and continue the game.

I felt sorry for the girls, who were losing the game. But they were having so much fun they didn't want to stop. During the game, the referee blew his whistle and told Annie she was offside.

"Should I go off the ice?" she asked.

He smiled. "No, it simply means you crossed the blue line before the puck did. Now we will have a face-off near the blue line."

The game resulted in a shutout with the girls losing by a score of 9-0. Everyone had fun, and the girls asked for a rematch on their rink.

After they lined up and shook hands, Shirley skated over to the boards where I was standing and hugged me. "Why didn't you play for the boys?"

I blushed. "I don't know how to skate well enough. I'm practicing though, so maybe next time I'll be on the team."

I watched as she skated away with her white figure skates.

She looked funny as she bobbed up and down with every stride. Back then, I didn't know figure skates were made different than hockey skates. Even though she skated funny, I admired her because she was like a big sister to me. In our Indian way, she was my big sister.

At seven o'clock on Saturday evening, we watched *The Hanging Tree*, a Western. The movie was about a doctor who rode into a small town called Skull Creek, Montana, to set up a doctor's office. He passed by the hanging tree, which was an old oak tree with a thick branch where a rope with a frayed end, presumably a former noose, still hung.

Near the end of the movie, the townsfolk had a riot. They carried the doctor to the hanging tree, tied his hands, and stood him up in a wagon bed with a rope around his neck.

The heroine named Elizabeth had struck it rich and offered all the gold she had to the townsfolk if they would let the doctor live. When she turned to walk away, the doctor called out her name. She returned to the wagon where he knelt, and they kissed.

The ballad playing in the background was sung by Marty Robbins and I couldn't get that song out of my head for the longest time.

Right after the movie, we made our way to the dorm. As we headed up the stairs, we talked about the scenes we liked in the movie.

Norman said, "I knew the doctor wasn't going to be hung because he was the 'main guy' and they never die.

He's like the Rawhide Kid who gets shot but never dies."

I told him, "Sometimes cowboys die."

Then he said, "Some do but not the main guys. Just watch *Bonanza* and you'll see."

So, I waited for *Bonanza* to come on and he was right. The Cartwrights had some close calls, but none of them ever died. I couldn't understand why all of their mothers died if good people didn't die.

In class, our grade-one teacher, Ms. Sedeski, wasn't as mean as some of the nuns and other staff members. She had more patience and I never saw her pull anyone's ears or pinch their cheeks the way the nuns did.

When we were seated at our desks, Ms. Sedeski congratulated us on our performance at the Christmas concert. "I'm very proud of the way you danced."

I crossed my fingers and hoped she wouldn't bring up my mistake of almost picking the wrong dance partner during our performance. But she never said anything about it.

When I glanced back at Sandra, she smiled at me and I blushed. I knew she remembered my mistake and how she stepped forward when I needed help.

Then Ms. Sedeski handed out some new books for everyone to put their names on. They were purple and *Phonics* was written across the front of them. She told us we would be getting more books like this when we finished all the work in this first book.

She said, "This book will teach you how to read and write properly. You will have a spelling test after you complete each section." So, phonics and spelling tests became a pattern for this period.

There were times I earned a gold star for getting all the words right, but other times I received a silver star for having one or two mistakes.

Ann, Maxine, and Sandra were always getting gold stars on their tests. They were smart and remembered how to spell all the words in each section.

Going to school was about competing against one another. For some students, learning came naturally. For others like me, the work was a little harder.

In this new class, we learned about grammar, but we also read stories such as "Cinderella," "Goldilocks," "The Three Little Pigs," and "Jack and the Beanstalk" whose real name was Jack Spriggins.

I enjoyed listening to the stories, especially when Ms. Sedeski had us sit on the floor in front of her.

She showed us pictures as she read the stories. She read slowly and carefully pronounced each word while emphasizing certain words to make the story more exciting.

During the story of "Cinderella," I was caught up in a fantasy world where Cinderella went to a ball and was the centre of attention for the evening. I smiled when she married the prince and left her mean stepmother behind.

That day, I learned I could lose myself in books and be happy in a make-believe world.

When we were back in the playroom, Mr. Gilbert told us the grade-one students would be lining up to get their haircuts in "The Block".

I didn't mind getting my hair cut, but I didn't like the new look it gave me: my ears looked like they were too big for my head.

When we arrived at the woodworking shop, I noticed our usual barber, Mr. Batza, was away, so Mr. Lang was taking his place and cutting our hair.

I hardly knew Mr. Lang other than seeing him in the office when I broke his picture window and when he was the master of ceremonies at the Christmas concert.

When it was my turn to sit in the barber's chair, I sat as quietly as I could. Did he remember I was the one who broke his picture window? Then I felt a sharp pain on the top of my right ear and I felt blood running down the side of my face.

He yelled at me, "Why did you move?"

We both knew I never moved.

He cut me on purpose. So that was his story and he stuck to it. He escorted me to the school nurse and blamed it all on me. What could I say when I was only a little boy and the school principal was telling lies about me?

I told myself we were even and I wouldn't feel guilty about breaking his picture window anymore.

Dishonesty thrived at Marieval along with a very strict code of conduct enforced by mean-tempered nuns, priests, and staff members.

I did everything possible to avoid upsetting them.

They would pinch my cheeks and pull my ears at every opportunity that came their way.

Like every little boy, I was curious, and sometimes, my curiosity got the best of me.

One day, my friend Randy, who was a day scholar, asked me to go into "The Block" with him. He wanted to buy a pop from the machine located in the basement.

I knew the pop machine was out of bounds, but the front door was unlocked, and I could imagine how good a cold pop would taste.

We quietly opened the door and tiptoed down the steps to the pop machine.

Randy said, "I'll put a quarter into the machine. If we both pull on pop at the same time, we might get a free one."

After trying it, we ended up losing his money. We tried shaking the machine and were in the process of kicking and tilting it when Sister Andre appeared out of nowhere.

Before we could explain what happened, she grabbed us by the ears and lifted us on our tiptoes. She took us upstairs to one of the classrooms. "Put your hands on the desk!"

Once we had done as she ordered, she hit our fingers several times with a yardstick.

I was sure she was going to break or dislocate one of my fingers. That would have meant another visit with the school nurse, and for some reason, it would have been my fault again. I was glad when she tired out, but it was a painful experience.

By the time she was done, my fingers were red and sore. She handed us each a piece of chalk. "Write this line on the board until I tell you to stop: I am a bad boy for stealing."

We each filled up a blackboard with the lines while she sat there and supervised us. We had to stand on chairs to reach the top of the blackboards. But, when we were done, she warned us, "The next time you try to steal something, I'm going to take you to the principal's office for the strap."

My fingers and hands ached as we headed back to the playroom. *Oh well, at least she didn't make me cry.*

Randy and I sat quietly on the benches, thinking about what happened.

As we sat there licking our wounds, we listened to the music coming from the radio. They were playing "Are You Lonesome Tonight?" by Elvis Presley. It was a nice song, but it reminded me of Mom and Dad.

I wondered if they were listening to this song. Every time one of the supervisors turned on the radio in the playroom or on the speaker outside, Elvis was singing his new song.

He was in the spotlight, and everywhere he went, girls screamed and chased after him.

While watching television one evening, one of the boys said, "Hey, you guys, Elvis Presley is in this movie."

It was a Western called *Flaming Star*. In that movie, Elvis was the son of a Kiowa mother and a Texas rancher father. His family, including a half-brother, Clint, lived on the Texas frontier. Life became chaotic for his family when a tribe of Kiowa Indians began raiding their neighbours. Elvis was caught between two worlds, the Indian world and the white world, but he belonged to neither.

I could relate to his situation. At Marieval, it was wrong to be an Indian, but on the other hand, I couldn't be a white boy. At the end of the movie, Elvis got shot and died.

My friends talked about that movie after watching it, and they wondered if it would be coming on again.

They were disappointed when they checked the television listings but couldn't find it anywhere.

Shortly after watching that movie, Mr. Gilbert turned off the television and said, "It's time to polish your shoes."

He placed a blanket in the center of the playroom floor that contained several cans of black and brown shoe polish along with different shoe brushes.

Some of the senior boys used one kind of brush for applying the polish and another kind for making their shoes shine. When a senior boy was done shining his shoes, he held up a brush and asked the others, "Who wants a shiner?"

The others looked at him and laughed. As usual, the junior boys had to wait for their turn to polish their shoes.

When most of the boys were done, it was my turn.

I polished one shoe, put it down on the blanket, and began polishing the other shoe. I was so busy talking with Norman I didn't notice I was getting polish on my pants. I held a newly polished shoe on my knee while working a good shine on the other side of it. Then I noticed my knee was black, the same colour as my shoes.

When Mr. Gilbert noticed my pants, he told me I was going to stay that way until we changed our clothes on Saturday night. I would have to go to class and the dining room with polish on my pants.

When we went up to the junior boys' dorm that evening, Grandma Smoker asked, "What happened to your pants?"

"I was polishing my shoes and accidentally got polish on my pants. I may have to stay like this until we change our clothes on Saturday."

She smiled and said, "Change into your pyjamas and give me your pants."

I didn't see what she did with my pants because my bed was in the other room. However, the next morning when the lights came on and it was time to get up, I noticed my pants at the foot of my bed. They were clean and the polish stain was gone. I wouldn't have to go around for the rest of the week with polish on my jeans. I hoped Mr. Gilbert wouldn't notice my clean pants because I didn't want Grandma Smoker to get into trouble over it.

He must have forgotten about it because he never mentioned it again.

In class, Ms. Sedeski asked us, "Who knows what a president of the United States is and how he becomes president?" She explained about elections in the United States and how the leading candidate with the most votes would become the leader of the country. "I hope John F. Kennedy will be elected as the next president. He will be the first Catholic president of the United States."

At the time, I didn't know anything about politics, so it was hard to understand what she was talking about. Then I heard John F. Kennedy became the president of the United States on January 20th, 1961.

The supervisors and staff members were interested in politics, especially when it concerned the United States and

Canada. For weeks after the election, John F. Kennedy was in the news.

Watching television was a great source for news and entertainment at Marieval.

The television show *Jungle Jim* was too scary for me to watch. I didn't yet understand the difference between reality and Hollywood's version of it. This show had all the dangers of an African jungle and the music they played magnified the danger even more. The show came on at seven o'clock, and in the winter, it was already dark outside. But that didn't matter. I still went outside too afraid to watch *Jungle Jim*.

All of my friends preferred to stay inside and watch the program, so I had the whole rink to myself. I skated by the lights of the rink and stayed on the ice until my toes got cold and I had to go into the dressing room to warm up.

The whistle blew at eight o'clock and one of the supervisors came outside to lock the dressing room.

When he noticed me out there alone, he asked me, "Why are you skating by yourself?"

"I don't like watching *Jungle Jim* and I want to practice my skating so I can play hockey against the girls someday."

Later that week, we received a letter from Mom and Dad.

When Norman opened the envelope, he checked for money and smiled when he pulled out two five-dollar bills.

In her letter, Mom told us things were going well back home. There was a lot of snow this year and they had to ask Uncle Gordon to use his team of horses to pull our grandparents' car to the highway. Dad and Uncle Ernie shot an elk in the park, so they needed the car to transport it home. She asked how we were doing in school and told us to say hi to Ernest. Mom never really said much in her letters.

Both of our parents and maternal grandparents were former students of these boarding schools, so they knew what Norman and I were going through.

Mom had attended Lebret Indian Residential School until she finished the eighth grade.

Receiving that letter left us with a bittersweet feeling. We were lonesome, but the money cheered us up a little bit.

On Sunday morning when we were in catechism class, Sister O'Deil. came down to the church basement.

She said, "Fidel Castro has seized power in Cuba and declared himself to be a communist. Pray hard so President John F. Kennedy can stop him from taking over the United States and Canada. Fidel Castro doesn't believe in our religion, and Cuba has the Russians on their side. The situation looks very grim, so pray for the United States."

I had no idea who Fidel Castro was, but I had heard enough about John F. Kennedy to know he was a good guy.

Back then, my way of thinking was based on the idea that a person was either a good guy or a bad guy, and I always cheered for the good ones.

February 4th, 1961, was my birthday, and I turned seven years old. Our teacher said, "Today's Walter's birthday, so let's sing him a birthday song."

I put my head on my desk as they sang to me. I blushed and wasn't sure how to act. This was something new to me, and now, everyone knew it was my birthday.

During a recess in the playroom, some boys from my class said, "Let's give him the bumps." Once again, this was a first for me as I had never received the bumps before.

One of the boys grabbed my arm while another one grabbed my other arm. Two more boys grabbed my legs. They lifted me waist-high and bumped my butt on the floor while counting from one to seven.

When they finished giving me the bumps, I lay on the floor tuckered out from the whole ordeal. One of the boys pinched my arm and said, "A pinch to grow an inch."

In hindsight, I had seen other boys getting the bumps, but I didn't know what it was all about. Now I knew and would see it many more times after that in school.

In catechism class a couple of weeks later, our teacher said, "Lent is going to be starting this week. You should think of something to give up for Lent."

She told us, "Christ went into the wilderness to fast. While he was out there, the devil appeared to him and tried to tempt him to break his fast. But Christ told him to leave."

As she talked, I wondered what I could give up for Lent. I couldn't give up food or water as he did, but maybe I could give up jawbreakers. I hoped no one would offer me any during Lent. When I told my catechism teacher, I was giving up jawbreakers, she smiled at me.

Later on, that day, I heard on the news the Russians and the Americans didn't like one another. They talked about a space race with the Russians to see who could land a man on the moon first.

There was also a threat of war with Fidel Castro. He was friends with Russia and they possessed missiles.

A reporter on television described the events as they unfolded. He talked about an invasion called the *Bay of Pigs*, and I tried to imagine some pigs swimming around in a bay.

I wondered how those pigs got into that bay and how they were going to get them out.

"Communist" became a common term at Marieval. Although I didn't know the full meaning of the word, I knew they were bad people. However, not everything on television was so serious.

Hockey Night in Canada with Foster Hewitt came on every Saturday evening. Back then, there were only six teams in the National Hockey League. The six teams were the Boston Bruins, Chicago Black Hawks, Detroit Red Wings, Montreal Canadiens, New York Rangers, and the Toronto Maple Leafs.

I was fascinated with hockey and cheered for the Chicago Black Hawks because they had a large Indian emblem on the front of their jerseys. In particular, I liked Bobby Hull, Stan Makita, and Glenn Hall.

Bobby Hull had the most goals on his team. He was called the golden jet because of his blonde hair and his speed on the ice. He was also known for his wicked slapshot due to the curved blade he used. He had a younger brother, Dennis who would eventually play for Chicago.

Foster Hewitt said, "Bobby Hull terrifies the goalies when they see him streaking down the ice and letting his blistering slapshot go towards them. He leads the league in scoring and Chicago fans hope he will reach the 50th goal mark."

I also liked Stan Makita because he was their captain and often assisted Bobby Hull when he scored a goal.

Glen Hall was a terrific goalie for Chicago, and I often imagined being like him if I played goal for the junior boys.

In class, our teacher told us Easter would soon be here. The weather was warming up and a feeling of spring was in the air. She had us colour pictures of bunnies, Easter eggs, and flowers. She also had us weave colourful baskets to keep our candies, chocolates, and Easter eggs in at home.

We cut out pictures and taped them to the windows to make our classroom look festive.

Ms. Sedeski told us a story from the Bible about Jesus and how he was nailed to a cross so the gates of heaven would be open again. Then I realized that's why they have a picture of a man on a cross in the church and on my rosary.

Ms. Sedeski said we would be learning more about this in our catechism class, and some students in grades two and three would be receiving their first Communion.

During the lunch break, some boys talked about their plans for the Easter holidays.

We hadn't heard from Mom and Dad for a while, and I wondered if we would be going home for the holidays.

I talked to Norman about it and he said, "Don't worry. I'm sure they'll borrow our grandparents' car and come for us." I crossed my fingers and hoped he was right. If they came to get us, we would be going home for nearly two weeks. I was getting excited just thinking about it.

As Easter approached, I found myself discussing the holidays with my friends and getting more excited with each passing day.

Another week passed, and I could hardly contain myself at the thought of going home.

In catechism class on Sunday morning, our teacher talked about the Last Supper and the Crucifixion of Christ on the cross. "Easter isn't just about chocolate bunnies and Easter eggs. It's a celebration of Christ opening the gates of heaven so lost souls can enter."

We saw pictures of soldiers beating Christ and putting thorns on his head for a crown.

I couldn't imagine how painful it must have been for him to have nails driven through his wrists and feet and a lance piercing his side as he hung there dying.

Our teacher told us he rose from the dead three days later, and that made me feel better.

I laughed when the soldiers discovered he was not in the tomb where they left him.

Later that evening, we had a church service called *The Way of the Cross*. Our Parish Priest Father Dumont served Mass that evening. During the service, I watched as the procession made its way around the church, stopping in front of pictures where Christ fell on his way to Mount Calvary.

Father Dumont prayed out loud, and we were told to pray with him.

I still didn't know most of the prayers, but I did mumble along and say the parts I knew. The service was interesting. It didn't last very long, but my knees were sore from all the kneeling we had to do. I was happy when it was over and we could go back to our playroom.

At eight o'clock, we lined up for bed and went to the junior boys' dorm. Grandma Smoker told us to brush our teeth and put on our pyjamas. She also had us say some prayers with her.

After we were done, she permitted us to stay up for an extra half-hour to read our comics or visit with one another.

I went over to Norman's bed to talk to him before the lights went out. The thought of going home for the holidays had me so excited that I needed to talk to him.

Ernest saw us talking, so he came over. "The last day of class will be on Thursday because Good Friday is a holiday. Although most of the boys are going home for the holidays, I don't mind staying at school for Easter like I did last year."

We talked about our grandparents. Do they ever think about what it is like for us here?

Ernest said, "I'm sure they do. They both attended schools like this one. Grandpa went to an industrial boarding school, and Grandma went to File Hills Residential School."

Talking about home was making me lonesome, but I tried my best not to show it.

A short time later, our dorm lights blinked so we knew it was bedtime. I had a hard time falling asleep that night because I was worried about a ride home. I kept tossing and turning, and although I wasn't sure who it was, I heard someone crying in the dark and hoped it wasn't Norman.

The next day, the skin between my toes wouldn't quit itching. My toes were red and I couldn't stop myself from scratching them.

When I told Mr. Dennis about my foot, he told me to go to the nurse's office and let him know what she said about my foot. He said, "You might have a case of athlete's foot."

After a careful examination, the nurse confirmed what Mr. Dennis thought. "You have a case of athlete's foot, so you won't be able to skate or take showers for a while."

Good, I thought to myself, no more dreadful showers and avoiding the supervisors in there.

She put white powder on my foot as she said, "I want you to come and see me every day until it's better. Don't walk around barefoot because this infection is very contagious. You can give it to someone if you're not careful,"

I said I would give up jawbreakers for Lent. Could I change my mind and give up skating instead of jawbreakers?

I went back downstairs and told Mr. Dennis I had athlete's foot. Without acknowledging what I told him, he said, "Go line up for class."

In class, Ms. Sedeski had a nursery rhyme to teach us called "Hickory, Dickory, Dock." It sounded funny at first, but it had a catchy little tune I couldn't get out of my head.

Then she shared a song with us called "Mary had a Little Lamb." We all laughed when we saw a picture of a lamb following Mary to school.

By the end of the class, we were able to sing both of those songs. That cheered me up and I wasn't so worried about the Easter holidays anymore.

It snowed hard all week, so they opened the shed where the toboggans, ice scrapers, and shovels were kept. It was nice watching the snow mounds build up as they kept scraping the ice and shovelling the snow over the boards, but it was a lot more fun sliding down those little hills.

I helped some of my friends build a tunnel along the boards so we could hide from the other boys. It was cozy hiding inside the tunnel, so we dug a maze of them with a couple of different entrances on the west side of the rink.

Martin and I were crawling along in our tunnels one day when we felt the boards start to shake. We didn't know what was happening, but it didn't sound good. We decided to get out of there. But before we could escape, the snow came crashing down on us.

Some of the senior boys thought it would be funny to see the snow cave in on us.

We gasped for air, but our mouths and noses were full of snow, and we were struggling to breathe. We almost suffocated before we got out of there.

When I could see daylight, I looked around for Martin, but he had already made his way out. I could hear some senior boys laughing.

They were the ones who caved in our tunnels. "You guys looked funny when you were struggling to get out of there."

"It wasn't funny for us! We nearly suffocated!" Our tunnels were ruined.

Our last day of school was on Thursday, March 30th, and Ms. Sedeski wished us a happy Easter. For those travelling far, she told us she would pray to St. Christopher who was the patron saint of travellers. She told us to have a safe trip home. Then she dismissed us for our Easter holidays

Many of the students left the school right after class while the rest of us waited anxiously for our parents to come and pick us up.

At four o'clock, Mr. Dennis brought us lunch and told us to wait in the playroom in case someone came to pick us up.

Shortly after that, more students left until there were only a few of us left in the playroom. I kept watching the clock, wondering if Mom and Dad were coming to get us.

By supper time, we were still waiting, and it was getting dark outside. We ate our supper in silence because we were afraid, we would be spending our Easter holidays here.

Ernest tried to cheer us up by sharing some fun things they did last year, but I could tell Norman wanted to cry.

I couldn't blame him because I felt the same way.

After our evening meal, Mr. Gilbert permitted us to go outside and skate because it didn't look like any more parents were coming that day.

I tried my best not to cry, but when I saw tears streaming down Norman's face, I burst into tears as well.

It was a very long and lonely evening, and we didn't know what to say to one another. The loneliness worsened when it was time for bed.

Mr. Gilbert told us we would be sleeping in the senior boys' dorm, and he assigned us a bed to sleep in for the night.

As it turned out, I was going to be sleeping next to Ernest, which wasn't so bad after all.

Before the lights went out, I talked with Norman.

He said, "Mom and Dad will come for us tomorrow."

"But what are we going to do if they don't come?"

"Don't think like that! You might make it come true."

I knew he was thinking of the same thing and didn't want to admit it. I felt like crying and didn't know what to say.

When we woke up the next morning, Norman and I were both worried and lonesome. We didn't want to spend our Easter holidays at this jail. We wanted to go home.

Ernest seemed to be more accepting of things as they happened. Maybe because he experienced being stuck here at school before and had lower expectations. His biggest concern was wondering what kind of fish they were going to serve us in the dining room. It was Good Friday, which was a statutory holiday.

I wanted to be at home like the other students who started their holidays yesterday.

Without checking our beds, a supervisor told us to bring our pyjamas and bedding down to the laundry room.

At the time, I assumed we would be exchanging our sheets for clean ones. I couldn't figure out why we didn't have to take clean sheets back upstairs.

After breakfast, I went to see the health nurse. She treated my foot and gave me a bottle of foot powder to use twice a day. She said, "Make sure to rub powder between your toes and sprinkle some inside your sock. Don't get your feet wet or walk around barefoot."

I assured her I understood and thanked her.

When I returned to the playroom, Father Carriere came downstairs and beckoned us to come with him to the parlour. "Your parents are here to pick you up," he said.

So, that's why we didn't have to take clean sheets back upstairs! Happiness flooded through me.

I looked at Norman and Ernest, who were both grinning at each other. It was a huge relief knowing we were going home for a few days and leaving this miserable place behind. I could hardly wait to see our family again.

As we entered the parlour, Mom and Dad were standing beside one another smiling at us. We stood there awkwardly, waiting for Shirley to come and join us.

I asked Mom, "Why didn't you come for us yesterday?"

She said, "Grandpa's car was in Joe Dubey's garage in Carlyle for repairs, and it was too late to come for you once the repairs were done. We phoned from town to let the school know we were coming for you today. I'm surprised they didn't let you know."

Father Carriere overheard our conversation but didn't say anything. Instead of explaining he ignored us. It was almost like we were shadows on the wall. After all, how many people talk to their shadows?

As we stood in the parlour, I asked Ernest if he still wanted to stay at the school like he did last year.

He said, "I'd rather be at home with our grandparents than being stuck here at Marieval. It is a lot more fun at home."

Mom laughed and told him, "Make sure you want to come home with us rather than changing your mind when we are partway home."

When she said that we all looked at Ernest and had a good laugh. The laughter broke the awkward silence in the room.

When Shirley came into the parlour Father Carriere spoke to Dad and reminded him to bring us back on Sunday, April 9th. He told us to enjoy our holidays and have a safe trip on our way to White Bear.

Chapter 7 - Home for Easter

As we approached the parking lot, I looked around for Grandpa's blue 1954 Ford, but it wasn't anywhere in sight. Instead, I saw a 1956 green Ford Sedan.

Mom said, "It's a better car but not as spacious as the older one. I'm going to miss that old car because it had a lot of good memories, like the times we went to pow-wows in the states and rodeos in Kennedy."

When we started to drive away from the school, Shirley asked Dad if the radio worked.

He told her it worked, but when he turned it on, the reception in the valley was poor. All we could hear was static, so he turned it off.

The drive to Broadview was slow going because of deep ruts on the gravel roads, but once we got to the blacktop highway, we were able to pick up speed. The weather wasn't bad, but as we drove past Broadview, it started to snow.

Shirley asked, "Are we going to make it home okay?"

Dad assured her we would be home around supper time.

When we arrived at our grandparents' place, Mom told us they moved back into the old log shack because it was a bit crowded in our grandparents' two-bedroom house.

As I was taking my coat off, I noticed the can of foot powder in my pocket, so I told Mom about my foot and what the health nurse told me to do.

She replied, "You'll have to keep reminding me because my memory is good, but it's rather short."

Then she smiled at me when I gave her a puzzled look. Oh, it was good to be home again.

The next day, we tagged along with Mom and Dad when they went to town. Surprisingly, Dad dropped us off at the show hall while they shopped for groceries and took them home. It was exciting going to a show and joining others who were interested in watching Western movies.

Dad said, "Wait outside the show hall when the movie is over and I'll pick you up there."

I smelled the aroma of fresh popcorn while we waited in line to buy tickets, and it reminded me of the bazaar.

Before the movie started, I glanced around the hall and noticed how many white kids there were at the show. It felt weird because there were more white kids than Indians. I was used to being at Marieval where all the boarders were Indians.

It didn't take long for the lights to dim and the show to begin. I felt safe the priests and nuns would never find us inside the coziness of this dark show hall.

They were showing a Western movie called, *The Magnificent Seven*. It was about a bandit who terrorized a small Mexican farming village.

Several of the village elders sent three of the farmers into the United States to search for gunmen to defend them. They ended up with seven, each of whom came for a different reason. They prepared the town to defend themselves against an army of thirty bandits who arrived wanting food. It was an exciting show, even better than *Jesse James*.

When the movie was over, we followed the crowd to the exit signs and found our way out to the main street where Dad was waiting for us.

He smiled. "Did you enjoy the show?"

"It was a nice movie. The popcorn tasted better than what I had at the bazaar." I don't know if it tasted better. Maybe the situation was better, so the popcorn tasted awesome.

When we got home, Mom took care of my foot. She told me to pull up a chair near the table where the coal oil lamp was shining the brightest and carefully inspected my foot before applying the foot powder.

As we sat at the table, Norman helped Dad bring in more wood from outside. Dad added some wood to the stove and carefully placed a couple of bigger green logs into our airtight heater. He said, "Green logs burn slower and last longer so I won't have to keep adding more wood to the fire."

By this time, it was getting late. When I peeked out the window, I could see the lights go out next door and knew our grandparents were going to bed.

Not long after that, I wondered why Mom and Dad were still sitting at the table after they put us to bed. Then I heard the sound of bottles clinking, and knew they were drinking. Dad must've dropped off some beer when he brought our groceries home from town.

I didn't mind them drinking as long as they didn't start arguing or fighting. I must've dozed off, but when I woke up, I saw Mom sleeping on the bed.

Dad was sitting up drinking. Since he didn't have anyone to converse with, he sat at the table singing pow-wow songs.

I listened to him for a while, and in a way, I was happy to hear pow-wow songs again.

When he drank up the last of his beer, he put more wood in the stove and turned off the lamp before going to bed.

Mom and Dad had their bed while I snuggled between my brothers on another bed. The fire crackled and the winds outside howled. Through the darkness, I glimpsed shadows from the fire as they danced around the room. The smell of the wood smoke floated through the room while I listened to the soft breathing of my brothers as they slept.

After breakfast, Norman asked Dad, "Do you have any snare wire we can use to catch rabbits for Mom?"

"I have some, but I hope the rabbits are still good to eat."

I asked, "How can you tell if a rabbit is good or not?"

"I'll show you if you catch any rabbits today."

We picked up Ernest before going to the bush to look for rabbit trails. We laughed at one another as we struggled through snow that was still quite deep in a few places. It was hard and crusty on top, but it was easy to fall through up to our knees. We tried shuffling along the top of the snow, but in certain spots, we were too heavy to stay on top.

Ernest said, "Grandpa talked about deer that would cut themselves on crusted snow, especially when running away from wolves or bears. When this happened, they were easy to track by the blood trail they left in the snow. The moose have it rough during the spring too because they are bothered by wood ticks. He shared times when they skinned a moose in the spring and found hundreds of ticks on them."

Out of curiosity, Norman asked, "Ernest, how can you tell if rabbits are still good to eat?"

"I don't know, but I'm sure Grandpa would know."

That evening, we were excited when we caught two rabbits in our snares. We watched as Mom skinned the rabbits and told us they were still good to eat. We were glad we didn't waste any rabbits, but that still didn't satisfy our curiosity. "How do you know?"

Mom told us, "I check the rabbits carefully and look for boils on their skin. If I find a boil on it, I'll throw it away and tell you to take your snares out of the bush."

The next day Dad borrowed Grandpa's car and told us to come with him for a ride. We were going to see if the northern pike in the northwest corner of the reserve were spawning yet.

We had a long trek from the #9 highway to the spawning site, but when we got there, the ice was still frozen along the shoreline.

Dad said, "The fish won't be spawning for a few more days. Once the ice melts along the shore, the females find their way to our slough and lay their eggs. That's when they are easy to catch."

On our way home, we drove by Carlyle Lake and watched some people pulling an ice shack towards the shore.

Dad remarked, "In the next few days, all the fishing shacks will be off the ice. The ice is getting too thin to leave them out there."

As we drove home, Dad shared a time he was riding in a truck with a friend and the truck started to go through the ice.

"We panicked when we couldn't get our doors open because the ice on the outside prevented us from opening them. We barely forced them open wide enough to jump out of the sinking truck. If someone was sitting in the middle, they would have gone down with the truck."

When we played outside during the winter, we were warned not to stick our tongues on the steel rain barrel, or anything else made of steel.

Mom said, "When Shirley was a little girl, she licked that steel barrel to see what would happen. Her tongue got stuck to it, and she was crying because she couldn't get it off. It was a good thing Ernest was outside playing with her. When he saw what happened, he got scared and raced inside to let everyone know Shirley's tongue was frozen to the barrel. Grandpa went outside with hot water from the kettle on the stove. He slowly poured hot water on the inside of the barrel until she could get her tongue off."

We sat there listening to Mom's story before I asked. "Then what happened, Mom?"

She looked around the table before replying, "When I examined Shirley's tongue, it was red with blood on the top of it. I reminded her of the warning I had given everyone."

Then Mom asked her, "What would've happened if there were no adults around? You would have been stuck like that for a long time. Shirley sat there that time with her hand over her mouth because she knew I was right."

The road from our grandparents' home to the #9 highway was a little more than a wagon trail. Near the house, it was often muddy when the ground thawed.

Grandpa planned on going to town for groceries on Saturday and wasn't sure if his car would make it up the hill the following morning.

So, on Friday evening he asked Dad to drive the car up the hill while the ground was frozen.

Dad took a run at the hill and made it to the top where he parked the car for the night.

The next morning, I was surprised when Mom said, "Grab your foot powder and come to town with us. The doctor needs to take a look at your foot to make sure it's healing properly. We don't want an infection to set in."

As we were getting ready to leave, the dogs started barking. Bobby Skeege, our neighbour, came running up to the car and said his mom was looking for a ride to town.

Back in those days, not too many people on the reserve owned cars. It was often difficult to catch a ride into Carlyle.

Dad told Bobby to get in and we would go and pick up his mom. It was an Indian squeeze, but we managed to get everyone into the car.

Grandma liked to visit Bobby's mom, Mary Maude because they were the same age and they always spoke to one another in Assiniboine. It was nice listening to them teasing one another or telling funny stories.

When we drove into town, we checked the mail before taking our grandparents to the store so they could shop.

Once we arrived at the store, Mom said, "Gary, push the shopping cart for us."

While we were in the store, Grandma and Mary Maude were standing at the meat counter. Mary Maude pointed to some sausages and said, "I'll take two dozen of those."

The butcher said, "I'm sorry I don't sell them by the dozen. I sell them by the pound."

She looked confused and told him, "Okay, then just give me one dozen."

Grandma laughed. "She doesn't speak very good English, so she doesn't understand what you mean." After saying a few words to Mary Maude in Assiniboine, Grandma told the butcher what to do. "Give her twenty-four sausages and charge her by the pound. She also wants half a dozen pork chops, a pound of sliced bologna, ground beef, a whole chicken, and a box of neck bones."

The butcher smiled. "You're in luck. I only have a couple of boxes left."

When it was Grandma's turn, she bought the last box of neckbones and more meat, before asking the butcher, "Do you have any beef or pork fat?"

He gave her a box of fat along with some dog bones.

"Mom, what is Grandma going to do with the fat?"

"She's going to make Indian popcorn for her soups".

Then Grandma asked Dad to drive her to the Abattoir to pick up some tripe because she loved to cook it and share it with her family and friends.

Our grandparents liked to stand in front of Forsythe's grocery store, milling around and visiting with their friends. While they were socializing in front of the store, Mom took me to the medical clinic for a quick checkup.

Once we were inside the clinic, Mom registered us with the receptionist even though there were only a couple of people ahead of us.

When it was our turn to see the doctor, he asked, "How did you get athlete's foot? How long have you had it?"

As he spoke, he removed my socks and carefully examined both of my feet.

Mom explained. "He had it when he came home from Marieval so he must have picked it up at school."

When he finished examining my feet, he told us, "As long as he continues using that foot powder, his foot will be better in a couple of days. There is nothing to worry about."

Looking at me, he asked, "Are you an athlete?"

I gave him a puzzled look, and he laughed, "If you were an athlete, there wouldn't be any cure for your condition because you would always have an athlete's foot."

Still laughing at his joke, he told Mom, "Make sure he doesn't walk around barefoot. Oh, and a follow-up appointment won't be necessary."

Mom thanked him for seeing us and assured him she would continue treating my foot until it was better. She looked relieved after we visited the doctor. "How are you feeling?" she asked.

"I'm happy the athlete's foot is almost gone. Now I don't have to worry about giving it to anyone else. And I'll let the supervisors know I'm better when I return to school."

When we left the medical clinic, we met our grandparents in front of Forsyth's grocery store.

Dad asked Mom, "What did the doctor have to say?"

"His foot is almost better. The doctor said, as long as we continue to treat it with that foot powder, it should be healed in a couple more days."

As we stood on Main Street, Percy came by with a brown paper bag under his arm.

Grandpa asked him, "What's in your bag, Percy?"

He smiled at Grandpa and said, "Groceries."

As soon as he finished saying that, his paper bag ripped open and a pig's head went rolling down the sidewalk.

Everyone burst out laughing because Percy looked funny chasing his rolling pig's head. To make matters worse, his bag was too damaged to hold his pig's head.

So, he placed it on top of his box of groceries inside the window of Forsyth's grocery store. He would have to leave his groceries inside the store until he could find a ride home.

I watched our grandparents and their friends laughing and pointing at Percy's pig's head that was sitting in plain sight of people passing by the store.

They couldn't stop laughing and pointing at it for the longest time. They kept teasing Percy, who blushed and headed to the bar in the Carlyle Hotel.

"Mom, how is Percy going to eat that pig's head?"

"He's probably going to make head cheese out of it. We've heard of him making his own before."

The weather was warming up and the days were getting longer. Our holidays passed too quickly. Before long, we would have to go back to Marieval.

In the evenings, Dad checked the shorelines to see if the fish were spawning yet. This was probably one of the few times I saw him fishing.

He said the fish were easy to catch because they swam into a slough on the reserve and spawned in large numbers. He talked of a wooden bridge they had constructed over a small stream so the fish passed below them.

"Last year, the game wardens watched helplessly because they couldn't stop the fish from spawning on the reserve. Once the fish swam onto White Bear, the game wardens couldn't stop us from fishing them out of the water, and they provided a feast for us."

We didn't need to be reminded to bring in our snares and split more wood so Dad and Grandpa wouldn't have to do it for a while.

During our final evening at home, Grandpa told Dad, "Park the car on the hill so you won't have any problems getting out of the yard when it's time to take the kids back."

We were sad knowing we wouldn't be coming home again until our summer holidays.

I wished we didn't have to go back to that awful place.

On Sunday, April 9th, when we were on our way to school, Dad gave us five dollars each.

Norman asked if we could stop at Mr. Leost's store to buy some treats before they dropped us off at school. It was nice to have money, but I would have gladly given it up for a chance to be going home with them.

I took my time looking around in the store because I wasn't in a hurry to return to school. I figured if I took my time, I would be spending a bit more time with our parents.

Finally, Dad said it was time to go, so I picked out a couple of comics and a bag of assorted candies, most of which were jawbreakers. Back then, you could buy three jawbreakers for a penny and a comic book for twelve cents.

I didn't see what Shirley and Ernest bought, but I knew what Norman bought: a tube of Brylcreem.

Chapter 8 - Back to That Horrible Place

After Mom and Dad left, we sat quietly on the benches in our playroom. We didn't feel like doing anything. There was a religious program on TV and we could hear a preacher talking about the Lord and his apostles.

He said the apostles were scared when Christ died on the cross. They could hardly believe it when he rose from the dead. One of them called, Thomas was so doubtful he refused to believe Christ was alive unless he could put his fingers in the nail holes in the Lord's wrists and feet.

We sat there listening to the preacher because the other channel was full of static.

Some boys were outside on the playground but they were probably hanging out in the dressing room. Not everyone was back at school yet, so most of the junior boys sat on the benches in the playroom feeling lost and lonely. Some were crying and wishing they were at home with their parents.

I didn't feel like going outside. I was sad because I was already missing Mom and Dad. Why did we have to go to school here? This place was not meant for us. It should be full of students who wanted to become nuns and priests. It could also be used for cadets, and basic training but not little Indian boys who needed to be with their parents. I recalled

Dad talking about his military training and Uncle Ernie's stories about jails in Regina and this is what this place sounded like to me.

While we were having our afternoon lunch, one of the supervisors said, "You have classes tomorrow, so this evening everyone will be taking a shower and sleeping in their respective dorms tonight. Furthermore, after lunch, you will be going up to your dorms to change your clothes."

Then I realized it was Sunday and *Bonanza* was on television this evening. Our parents didn't have electricity. I don't think anyone else did either, except for Mr. Anderson, the Indian agent who lived down east. Although I was lonesome, I looked forward to watching *Bonanza* again.

After changing my clothes, Mr. Dennis told me to go and see the health nurse to have my feet checked for athlete's foot. "We don't want you to spread it to the others, and we need to know if you can have a shower this evening."

"Sir, I saw a doctor in Carlyle, and he said my feet were healed." But he didn't hear a word I said.

He told me to let him know what the nurse said.

I didn't want to get him upset so I made my way up the stairs and knocked on the nurse's door. When she heard me knock, she told me to come in.

After carefully examining my feet, she said, "You won't have to see me anymore as long as you don't catch it again."

I asked her, "Can I have a shower with the others?"

She thought about it before saying I was no longer contagious. Now I wouldn't have to worry about keeping something on my feet when I used the washroom at night.

Oh good, I'd be able to skate again, at least that's what I thought. But when I went outside, I was surprised to see the ice was soft and starting to melt.

The only hockey left for this season was going to be on television during the Stanley Cup playoffs. However, there was still a bit of snow left on the hills, so maybe we could go sliding one more time before it all melted away.

While I was out on the playground, there wasn't a supervisor around, so I joined a group of boys who were walking on the top of the rink boards. It was fun seeing how far I could walk before I lost my balance and had to jump to the ground.

I looked around to make sure the coast was clear before giving it one final attempt. I walked a few feet on top of the boards then lost my balance.

As I fell, both of my feet went in opposite directions, and my crotch landed on top of the boards. I fell to the ice, rolling around and writhing in agony.

A blackness came over me, and I lost my breath for a while. Tears were streaming down my face, but I couldn't cry because my breathing came in short gasps. I moaned and held my crotch as I rolled around on the ice.

A boy stood over me. "Are you alright?" he asked.

I couldn't answer right away, that's when I heard him say he was going to get a supervisor. I managed to stop him when I said, "No, don't. I'll get into trouble for walking on top of the boards."

He said, "Okay I won't."

I tried to stand up, but it hurt too much, so I just stayed on my knees and cried for a while. By now, I knew more boys were getting scared, and they didn't want to get into trouble for not reporting the accident.

They waited for a few more minutes then they helped me to my feet and held on to my arms to steady me.

I kept holding my crotch while taking shallow breaths. I hung onto the boards and slowly made my way towards the dressing room.

A sigh of relief come over my friends' faces after I sat on a bench and told them I was going to be alright.

It doesn't take long for word to get around, especially fights or accidents, so in a few minutes, Norman and Ernest came rushing into the dressing room.

"What happened? Do you want to go see the nurse?"

"I can't do that because I'll get into trouble for walking on top of the boards."

"Can you walk?" Norman asked.

"I can, but it hurts when I walk. I just want to sit still"

They decided to let me rest until the whistle blew and it was time to go inside.

I tried my best to walk normally when Mr. Gilbert watched us come inside. I think he was suspicious about my timid steps, but he didn't say anything. My private parts were very sore, but I sat quietly in the playroom until I started to feel better. I certainly wasn't going to do that again

After washing my hands for supper, I asked Norman, "Can I have a little dab of your Brylcreem? I like the way it smells and how it makes my hair shiny."

So did the senior boys who took extra time to put it in their hair and slick it back.

Now I knew why Norman asked Dad to stop at Mr. Leost's store before they dropped us off earlier. He wanted to buy Brylcreem for his hair.

I couldn't remember him buying anything else.

Today, the senior boys took longer than usual getting ready for supper, so by the time they were done, it was almost time for us to line up.

Mr. Gilbert scolded us for taking so long in the washroom, and he looked at the junior boys when he said that. It wasn't like we had much choice as the senior boys used the sinks and mirrors before we did, but I'm sure he knew that. It felt strange being back at this lonely school.

Once again, thoughts of running away came to my mind. Maybe if I asked Norman, we could make it home together. But when I mentioned it to him, he said, "If they catch us, we'll get the strap." So that was the end of my plan.

I hated the Indian agent, Mr. Anderson, for sending us here. I also resented all the mean people who worked here.

In the dining room, so many girls were staring at us that my face flushed. I just wanted to eat and get out of there. I didn't feel hungry. Besides, I still had some candies in my pocket and they tasted better than the goulash and mashed potatoes we had for supper. I forced myself to eat the food on my plate because I knew we were being watched.

When we were almost done eating, Sister Superior rang her bell and ordered us to finish eating in silence. I wondered if she had to eat the last part of her meal in silence.

I was happy when we were dismissed from the dining room and allowed to go back to our playroom. I had to use the washroom and there was hardly anyone in there except for an older boy. Unfortunately, I had met him before and he was a bully.

He watched me as I washed my hands and kept staring at me. He said, "How are you doing you ugly bugger?"

At first, I thought he was joking, so I smiled and kept washing my hands. Before he left, he shoved me and glared at me like he was planning how he was going to hurt me.

I don't know what made him do that. I instantly thought of some of the other boys who were always picked on and now it was my turn. Should I tell someone or would that make things worse? After giving it more thought, I decided to keep it to myself and stay out of his way. If things got worse, I would take him on and bust him up if I had to fight.

I remember Dad saying, "If someone picks on you, punch him in the nose, and it'll take the fight right out of him."

I went back to the playroom after that incident and saw Puchees coming in from outside.

His parents must have dropped him off a few minutes ago because he had a lot of candies, chips, and pop.

He smiled when he saw me and asked if I wanted to trade one of my comics that was sticking out of my back pocket for some of his candies. That was a tough decision, but I decided to swap him one of my comics for a bottle of pop.

Later that evening, Mr. Gilbert told us it was time for a shower. He pointed to some shorts in the centre of the playroom and told us to pick out a pair and take a shower. "I'm not going to turn on the TV until everyone is finished taking a shower."

I was relieved when none of the supervisors joined us in the shower. It was a welcome break for the junior boys.

As *The Ed Sullivan Show* came on, I sat in front of the TV. *Bonanza,* my favourite show, was coming on next.

The senior boys sat on chairs in a semicircle facing the TV, and the junior boys sat cross-legged on the floor in front of them. With this arrangement, I could stretch my legs and still be able to see the TV without bothering anyone.

I enjoyed watching Ben Cartwright and his three sons ride up to the front of the set on their horses. Little Joe's horse, a black-and-white pinto stallion, was fascinating.

Maybe someday, I would own a horse like that. I could just imagine myself racing along the valley with the wind blowing through my hair. If I owned a horse like that, nobody would be able to catch me. I would laugh and gallop away from the supervisors, nuns, and priests.

Once the show started, everyone was quiet. However, during the commercials, we all began to talk at once and shared what we liked about the action in the show. We forgot about our families back home and cheered for the Cartwrights as their story unfolded. We laughed at the bad guys and held our breath when things got serious.

I stared at the little red covered wagon that was on top of the TV. Who had made it? Where had it come from?

When *Bonanza* was over, Mr. Dennis turned on the lights and told us it was time for bed. He ordered us to line up according to our numbers and follow him upstairs.

As we got to the junior boys' dorm, I was expecting to see Grandma Smoker there. But instead, there was a nun, called Sister Mary sitting in her place. "Change into your pyjamas and get ready to say your prayers. Don't forget to brush your teeth and use the washroom."

After everyone was ready, she said, "Kneel beside your beds and repeat the prayers I recite for you." She stood in the corridor to watch both rooms and make sure we prayed along with her.

As soon as we finished praying, she said, "Climb into bed and go to sleep now. It's late."

I wished Grandma Smoker was at the school because she always gave us time to read our comics before turning the lights out.

As I lay in the dark, I thought of my new comic and how I had looked forward to reading it this evening. I tried to sleep but kept thinking of Mom and Dad and how much I missed them. I wanted to go home and never have to come back here again.

What did this place look like when Dad went to school here? That was a long time ago. Did it look different then? Who knows? He may have slept in this very room at one time; that was a comforting thought.

As I was dozing off, I heard someone crying. Before long, I could hear a couple more junior boys crying in the dark.

The next morning before breakfast, I looked around at the boys in the playroom. By now, I was starting to know their names and their personalities. I looked at Nick, Chester, Lawrence, Harry, Buddy, Bruce, Douglas, Tucker, Glen, Willie, Herbie, Urban, Cuddy, Froggy, Ning-Ning, John, Wiener, Mink eyes, Dennis and Silly Butcher.

I could tell by their confidence most of them had been at Marieval for years. Some of them had their hair slicked back with Brylcreem. Others wore clickers on the bottom of their shoes that made a clicking sound when they walked on the hard linoleum floors or the sidewalks outside. To make more of an impression, some had truckers' wallets in their back pockets that were attached to their belts by chains.

Once my thoughts came back to the room, I glanced at a senior boy who smiled at me. It wasn't a fake smile but a real, genuine smile. I didn't know his real name, but his nickname was Froggy and he was the one who fell through the ice when we went skating on the river.

I was sitting on a bench when he approached me and introduced himself. My name is John James but my friends call me Froggy because they say I'm bow-legged.

He sat beside me and started telling me about himself. He said, "I have two younger brothers going to school here. One is named Tucker and the other one is Glen."

He called them over and introduced me as his new friend. He said, "You're the one who broke Mr. Lang's window. The one called *Little Boxer*, right? What's your real name?"

I told them about the name mix-up. "Now everyone calls me Walter but my real name is Robert Gary."

He asked, "What are you doing after school? You want to meet me and Glen out on the playground?"

"Sure." I could tell he wanted to be my friend, and I was sure he would protect me.

Once that bully saw me hanging around with Froggy and his brothers, he would be too scared to pick on me again.

I made a promise to myself if he ever shoved me again, I would let my new friends take care of him. However, I was sure he saw me talking to Froggy because he stayed away from me after that. A huge burden had been lifted off my shoulders now that I had some new backers.

That morning, it felt strange lining up for our class after our Easter holidays.

Sister O'Deil came into our grade-one classroom and gave us another lecture. She told us what happens to those who die with sins on their souls. Some of the things she talked about we had already heard in our catechism classes.

The day scholars weren't in our catechism classes, so I think she wanted to make sure everyone knew about these teachings.

When she described what it was like in hell, it scared the daylights out of me. She told us about Lucifer, who at one time was a good angel in heaven, but he turned bad and now lived in hell. She described him as having horns instead of a halo. The people in hell were being burned by fire and had to stay there forever. It was hard to imagine what it would be like to live in a burning place like that. She said, "When you receive your first Communion, you'll be able to go to confession and have your sins forgiven."

Had I done anything wrong? I don't want to go to hell when I die. The only thing I could remember was breaking Mr. Lang's window and hanging from the pipes. Oh, and trying to get a free pop from the machine.

She explained the difference between mortal sin and venial sin. She said, "If you die with a mortal sin on your soul, you will go to hell. For a venial sin, you will go to purgatory. The Communion host is the body of Christ, and the wine the priest drinks is the blood of Christ."

I recalled Mom and Dad drinking wine after I went to bed. Now I knew why they drank wine with Uncle Ernie, and it made me feel better.

After class as we sat in the playroom, I looked for Froggy and saw him sitting with the senior boys. I wanted to give him something, but my comics were in the dorm. I decided I would save my apple for him since he was my new friend.

As we sat there, Mr. Dennis told us there was still snow on some of the trails around the school, and we could go sliding before supper.

As soon as we were dismissed, most of the boys went racing for the toboggans. By the time I got there, they were all taken, but Froggy was lucky enough to get one.

He said, "Go sliding with me."

"I don't like sitting in the front," I told him.

He laughed. "You won't have to sit in the front. I'll show you what I mean when we get to the top of this trail."

We walked up a different hill and I wondered how we could both sit in the back.

When we got to the top of the trail, he laid down on his tummy and told me to sit on his back and hang on.

He steered the toboggan with his feet. When we started to pick up too much speed, he would drag his feet and use them as brakes. This was the best toboggan ride I ever had.

When he asked me if I wanted to try it again, I said, "Yes!" We must have slid down that hill three or four times before we heard the whistle blow.

While we were going back to our playground, I noticed my apple in my pocket, so I offered it to him. It was my way of thanking him for all the fun I had sliding.

He smiled, pulled out a pocket knife, and cut it in half.

I was happy he shared that apple with me because I was hungry. Our lunch had been such a long time ago.

As we walked back, he asked, "What reserve do you come from? Who are your parents?"

I told him, "My parents are Norman and Hazel and they live on White Bear."

"I'm from Lestock. We have a herd of horses at our place. You'll have to come and see me during the summer holidays. We can ride horses together." Riding horses sounded like so much fun.

When we got back to the playroom, I told Norman about my adventures and how I was invited to ride horses during the summer holidays.

He smiled and said, "You should have told him I like to ride horses too."

"I'll mention it to Froggy the next time I talk to him."

During supper, Sister Superior said she had a surprise for us after we were finished eating. Right away, I thought about a nice dessert or something like that, but I was wrong.

When everyone was finished eating, she rang her bell and called for silence. She reached into the sleeve of her habit and pulled out a note.

Someone had written a love letter that was confiscated by the girls' supervisor. In the letter, this young boy told a certain girl how much he loved her and how he missed her during the holidays. He said he thought of her every night before he fell asleep. She was the love of his life, and to him, no other girl mattered because she was so beautiful. He talked about marriage and said he would be the one to change his last name when they got married.

Then Sister Superior asked everyone what H.O.L.L.A.N.D. meant. When no one answered, she looked at the boy who wrote the note and asked him what it meant.

He was blushing when he told her, "Hope Our Love Lasts And Never Dies."

Of course, everyone laughed. Both the boy who wrote the note and the girl whom it was addressed to blushed and put their heads down.

Sister Superior finished reading the note and asked everyone what T.A.R. meant.

One of the girls replied, "Tear After Reading."

By now, the supervisors had their door open and were joining in the laughter. Mr. Dennis, who was standing in their doorway, asked, "Is there a stamp on the note? I have some for sale in my office."

After the laughter died down, Sister Superior said, "There will be no more love notes passed around. If I find any more notes, I am going to read them for everyone in the dining room to hear."

At that moment, I was glad I was too young for girls, and more importantly, I was glad it wasn't my note. That must've been embarrassing to have the whole school laughing at you.

The weather was getting warmer and the snow was starting to melt. A group of boys made small boats and put them into little streams near the sidewalk. It looked like a fun thing to do, so I decided to join them.

I found a large twig, broke it in half, and threw it into a stream. It floated away, and I followed it as it made its way into a larger stream. I could hear water rushing in the creek near our playground. How fast would my little twig go in that rushing current? But that creek was off-limits, so I had to settle for the small streams on the playground.

Some boys were using their imaginations for making little boats. They were making them out of tree branches, shingles, or paper. When the boys raced one another, the lighter ones made out of paper won most of the races.

The snow here was melting. Were the fish spawning back home on White Bear? If so, our dad and our relatives must be having fun catching the fish as they spawned.

I went to a spot in the northwest corner of our reserve with Dad last year where the fish were plentiful.

At the time, we stood on a footbridge where we could see the fish coming toward us by the dozens. It was amazing to see so many of them swimming together.

Dad would toss one of them through the air and watch it flop around on the river bank. It didn't take him long to catch enough fish for our family, grandparents, and friends.

It was a long walk back to the #9 highway and Dad had to stop and rest many times because the fish he caught were heavy. His back was wet, slimy and full of fish scales but he didn't seem to mind. He referred to it as all in a day's work.

Everyone was thankful for the fresh fish they received, and none of it was wasted.

It was fun watching Mom and Grandma scale the fish and pull out all the fish eggs. Mom cooked some of the fish in a frying pan and warned us to be careful of the bones when we ate them.

I looked toward the dam and wondered when will the fish here would be spawning. I asked one of my friends if he knew but he told me he didn't know. Maybe catching the fish as they spawned here was not a big deal for his family.

Later that evening when we went to bed, Grandma Smoker was back from her holidays, and she smiled when she saw us coming through the door. By now, I knew the routine, so I quickly brushed my teeth, put on my pyjamas, and knelt by my bed while we prayed.

Then I reached for the comics I kept stashed under my pillow. I wanted to read my newest one so I could trade it to someone in the morning for a different comic. I barely had enough time to finish reading it before the lights dimmed. I looked over at Ernest and Norman.

They were putting their comics away too.

It took me a long time to fall asleep because I was lonesome and wondering how much longer it was going to be before we could go home. I kept thinking about Mom and Dad and my younger siblings back home.

Before I dozed off, I thought about my new friends, who were all senior boys, and knew I wouldn't have to worry about getting picked on at school again. That was comforting to know. The days at Marieval were lonely times and I often thought of running away.

The nuns and the priests never hugged us or told us we were good boys. More importantly, no one ever told us they loved us. They only looked for our mistakes and were quick to punish us.

We would get our ears pulled for not moving fast enough. Not a day went by when we weren't being corrected or punished for something we did or did not do. Many of my days were spent living in fear I would make a mistake and get punished for it. It was worse now that I knew about sins and I was afraid of going to hell where the devil waited for me in a huge fire that burned forever.

Now that the warm weather had settled in, the ice was too soft for skating, but it was still hard enough for a game of broomball.

One afternoon, I stood along the boards and watched a group of senior boys playing broomball.

Tucker noticed me standing there and asked me to join them and be on their side. In a way, it was like playing hockey, but instead of a puck, we used a medium-sized black ball and we didn't wear skates.

We passed the ball around and tried to score on the goalie who was in the same net we used for playing hockey. Since it was a pickup game, there were about seven or eight players on each side. If anyone wanted to join the game, they were told to be on the side with the least number of players.

It was fun playing broomball because I had never played it before. I noticed it was hard to get traction on the ice and it was difficult to stop or turn without sliding. I didn't want to go into the corners because that's where the water pooled as the ice melted.

Mr. Dennis was on our side, but most of the good players were on the opposing side, so it seemed like they were always in our end.

I ran up the ice and lost my balance when I tried to stop. I fell backward and I could feel the back of my head hit the ice with a thud.

I was lying on the ice holding my head when Mr. Dennis came over and told me not to move. I could see the look of concern on his face as he asked, "Are you okay?"

It hurt so much I could feel tears welling up in my eyes.

He felt the back of my neck and head where a big lump was forming. "Can you move your legs?"

After a few minutes, he helped me to stand up, but I felt dizzy and told him I wanted to sit down.

He told the other boys to keep playing and he was going to take me to the playroom.

When we got there, I sat on one of the benches.

"Don't go anywhere," he said.

In a few minutes, he returned with a health nurse. She examined the lump on the back of my head and felt my neck before asking me if I felt dizzy.

When I told her, I felt weak and light-headed she told Mr. Dennis, "He needs to rest and take it easy as he may have suffered a concussion."

She gave me some medication to help with my headache.

I spent the rest of the day in bed and slept a lot because I felt so weak and tired.

When I woke up, I could hear voices and laughter. It was Norman and Ernest bringing me food from the dining room.

They brought me some apple juice, chicken soup, and Jell-O topped with ice cream.

I ate a bit of the soup and drank the juice but didn't feel like eating anything else.

Norman asked, "Can I have your dessert?"

Ernest said, "Hey, I was going to ask him for that."

They both laughed and agreed to share it; Norman ate the Jell-O and Ernest had the ice cream.

I was back on my feet the next morning.

Mr. Gilbert said, "I've posted a broomball schedule on the bulletin board for the senior boys. There will be a round-robin tournament starting on Friday, and the finals will be on Sunday. There will be prizes for the winners."

I could feel the excitement in the air as the boys began talking back and forth.

He continued, "I'm working on a junior boys floor hockey tournament to be held in the gym at the same time. As with the broomball tournament, there will be prizes for the winners. It will also be a round-robin format with the finals on Sunday. Check the schedule, and remember, this is about sportsmanship and having fun, but it is your responsibility to show up for your games. Good luck."

Mr. Dennis said, "Hopefully you learned from Walter's accident it can be dangerous playing on the ice."

What he said next was directed at me. "You aren't going to be playing in the tournament because floor hockey can be very physical, and I don't want to take a chance you will be further injured." He paused for a moment. "How are you feeling?"

"I'm okay, and I was hoping to play in the tournament."

Mr. Dennis sighed. "I will send you for a checkup before the tournament. If the health nurse gives you the okay, I will put you on one of the teams. But for now, you'll stay on the injured list."

The boys laughed when he said that, but I smiled because it made me feel important.

I had the occasional dizzy spell during the week, but the episodes were getting farther and farther apart. I hoped I would be well enough to play in the tournament because it sounded like fun, and I didn't want to be sidelined.

Friday morning, I crossed my fingers when I went to the nurse's office.

She carefully examined my eyes with a little penlight and pupil gauge. Then she checked my ears.

I told her about the floor hockey tournament, and she responded with a definite, "No way."

Then I thought of the leather helmets we had in the dressing room and told her I could wear one to play in the tournament.

"The answer is still no. It's far too risky. If you bang your head again, you could end up paralyzed and in a wheelchair."

I sadly went back to the playroom and told the supervisors I couldn't play in the tournament.

Later that afternoon, I watched the floor hockey game in the gym and cheered for the team Norman was on. I had time to watch and cheer for Tucker's broomball team before supper and it looked like they were having a lot of fun.

On Saturday evening, right after *Hockey Night in Canada,* we had to take a shower.

I figured out a plan for showering. Usually, the senior boys grabbed a faucet for themselves, so I quickly jumped into the shower and asked Froggy if I could share his faucet.

He said, "Sure thing, pal."

I didn't stay in there long, and before the supervisor came in, I was already getting out.

Sunday afternoon, I watched the floor hockey finals in the gym. It was a close game with my friend Steve's team winning the tournament. They received chips and pop, while the runners-up won treats as well.

The games were fun to watch and I looked forward to the day when I would be able to play in this tournament.

Out on the ice, Tucker's team, which was made up of mostly grade-eight students, won the broomball tournament.

Since both finals were happening at the same time, I missed the broomball game. But the broomball games I did watch looked like a lot of fun.

I laughed when Mr. Gilbert tried to use a toilet bowl plunger to get the broomball to stick to it. The ball wouldn't stick to the plunger, so he threw it into the net and used his broomstick.

The excitement from the tournament slowly subsided, and everyone turned their attention to *The Ed Sullivan* show followed by *Bonanza*. We never got tired of ending our week by watching this Western show.

On Monday morning, Ms. Sedeski smiled as we walked into the classroom. We started the morning by singing "O Canada" and "God Save the Queen." I knew both of these patriotic songs by heart because we sang them every morning before class.

After we were seated, our teacher pulled out a book with a picture of Humpty Dumpty on the first page. He was a cracked egg with skinny little legs sitting on a fence.

She told us a story of how he had a great fall and all the king's men and all the king's horses couldn't put him back together again. She showed us pictures as she read the story.

Then she had us take out our scrapbooks and told us to draw a picture of how Humpty Dumpty would look if he was back together again.

I tried my best to draw a picture of an egg with human parts, but I don't think it turned out very well, so I didn't bother showing it to anyone.

After lunch, she shared another story called "*Three Blind Mice*." She turned that story into a song and we all learned to sing it that day. Singing has a way of making a person feel better and singing "*Three Blind Mice*" did that for me.

Before we left the classroom, she asked who we thought was going to win the Stanley Cup this year. She surprised us because we didn't think she watched hockey.

Then I remembered she said her husband liked to watch the N.H.L. hockey playoffs on television. So, I figured she shared this common interest with him.

Later that evening, most of the senior boys watched the game on TV. The junior boys who weren't interested in hockey could always play cards or board games.

I watched the first part of the game then went out to the playground where I saw Froggy walking out to the football field. I caught up with him, and we talked about our plans for the summer holidays.

Froggy said, "My dad has been visiting relatives on Sakimay these past few days. You should come and meet him next weekend. He is related to your classmate Stanley."

"I would like to meet your dad and see where Stanley lives. I'm not sure if they'll allow me to leave school, but I'll ask and let you know by Friday. My biggest concern is Norman. I don't want to leave him and have him worry about me over the weekend."

We stayed outside until the whistle blew and it was time to go back inside.

When we were in the playroom, I asked Norman, "What do you think of me going to spend the weekend in Sakimay?"

He scratched his forehead like he always did when he was thinking hard. Then, he said, "But what if Mom and Dad come for a visit?"

"Gee, I never thought about that, maybe I'd better stay at school so I won't cause trouble for anyone. Mom and Dad would be worried if they came to visit us and I wasn't here." In a way, I was happy he warned me about it because I was not sure if I was ready to go and stay with strangers.

When we went to bed that evening, I decided to get Ernest's opinion. "Ernest, what do you think about me camping with friends from school for a weekend?"

He said, "Be careful who you go home with because some parents have drinking parties. Not all the students have good parents, and if you have to run away during the night, where would you go, especially if you didn't know where anyone else lives? Some of my friends asked me to go home with them, but I've always declined their offer so Shirley wouldn't worry about me."

That made a lot of sense because I remembered times on White Bear when drinking parties became violent, and the women and children had to find a safe place to go.

I made up my mind I would tell Froggy I had to stay at the school, at least until I was older and could take care of myself. I also told Norman what Ernest shared with me.

He looked relieved when I told him I decided to stay at the school instead of going home with Froggy.

While we were in class the following morning, Sister O'Deil knocked on our door and asked Ms. Sedeski if she could talk to us about the first Communion sacrament. She told us a bishop was coming from Regina in a couple of weeks, and she wanted to be sure everyone would be ready for his visit. She seemed nervous as she talked about the bishop and how we were to act in his presence.

She said, "I know you won't be receiving Communion until next year, but it is never too early to learn about it. You can't receive Communion until you've been baptized and you cannot receive Communion if you have sin on your soul. Therefore, everyone needs to go to confession and confess their sins to a priest inside the confessional."

I tried to imagine what it would be like to receive Communion. I already knew what my sins were: hanging on the pipes, breaking a window, and trying to steal a pop. I wasn't sure what kind of sins they were. Maybe hanging on the pipes was a small sin and breaking the picture window was a big sin because it was a big window. But I wasn't sure about the pop because I never got a free one.

After Sister O'Deil left the class, our teacher shared some more Mother Goose nursery rhymes with us.

She read one about a cow that jumped over the moon and showed us a picture of a milk cow flying through the air with a picture of the moon beneath her.

I didn't think cows could jump that high.

After recess, she shared another nursery rhyme, "*Baa, Baa, Black Sheep.*" That sheep had saved up three bags of wool for her master, her dame, and a little girl who lived down the lane. I had no idea how a person got wool from sheep, but it wasn't something I was too worried about.

The weather was still getting warmer and the days were getting longer. The ice and snow on the playground were disappearing fast. The only hockey games left for this season were the Stanley Cup playoffs. I liked to watch hockey on TV, but sometimes the games were so long I needed to take a break and go outside.

The boys raced one another on the swings to see who could go the highest. Some of them would go so high they nearly flipped over the top, but when they scared themselves, they would stop.

A couple of them wound up the chains of the swings tight and then let themselves go as the chains unwound. This looked like fun, but I decided not to try it because I knew it could make me feel nauseous and I didn't want to get sick.

I went back to the playroom and Steve asked, "Do you want to Indian wrestle with me?"

"I don't know. How is it played?"

He said, "Lay on the floor beside me with each of us facing opposite directions. Next, we lift our legs in the air. On the count of three, we lock our legs together and try to flip the other person over." Steve was bigger and more athletic than me, so on the first try, he flipped me over, and I nearly landed on my head.

He laughed. "Do you want to try it again?"

I said, no, because I recalled the nurse saying if I banged my head again, I could get another concussion. "Maybe it would be better if we just had a regular wrestling match."

So, he ended up getting me in a headlock, but my eyebrow got caught on one of the button-hooks on his farmer jeans. The hook was broken and a jagged part pierced my eyebrow. My skin was caught on that hook.

When he realized what happened, he let me go and helped me to get untangled from his jeans. A small amount of blood oozed from my eyebrow and he got scared. He begged me not to tell on him and helped me to the washroom so we could clean that cut. He kept apologizing, and I could tell he was scared he was going to get into trouble.

"You're my pal. I'm not going to tell a supervisor because I know it was an accident."

Steve was a natural rough guy, and sometimes his aggression got him into trouble.

As the days passed, the interest in the Stanley Cup games grew more intense. For one of the games, Mr. Dennis put a chart on a bulletin board with several squares on it.

For ten cents, you could buy a square which gave you a chance to win the raffle. You increased your chances of winning by buying more squares.

Once all the squares were sold, he filled in the chart with random numbers. For example, Chicago was at the top of the chart and Detroit on the side of that chart. Numbers were picked along the top and down the sides, and where the numbers intersected on a square that became your score for the game. Some of the scores were a bit high, while others seemed too low.

On Friday, the game ended with Chicago beating Detroit 6-3, and Wayne, who was one of the day scholars from Sakimay, had that square. He was going to be in for a pleasant surprise when he returned to school on Monday.

I watched part of the game then spent the rest of the evening out on the playground with Ernest and Norman.

While we were outside, we noticed an old panel truck pulling into the parking lot.

Ernest said, "Hey Puchees, your mom and dad are here."

Puchees went racing between the school and the white pump house. He hopped into the back of that panel truck before anyone could see him.

Ernest looked at me and said, "He's shy."

We laughed and went back to the playroom.

I told Froggy I wouldn't be able to go home with him in case my parents came for a visit, and he understood.

He told me he would probably stay at the school because he wasn't sure if his dad was still around. He never talked about his mom, so I wasn't sure if his parents were still together or not.

On Saturday, we went for a long walk along the valley. I was happy to know we wouldn't be climbing any steep hills. We started our walk by heading south toward the cut bank then followed a wagon trail heading west along the valley.

As we walked, we found an old buffalo skull half-buried in the ground. We showed it to Mr. Gilbert, who said, "That proves there were buffalo here at one time."

That old trail eventually met up with a gravel road and it went past old man Trottier's place. He was the shoemaker at the school, who repaired our shoes and made them as good as new again. His house looked cozy, but there didn't appear to be anyone home. There were two dogs in front of his house who kept barking at us. One of them looked like a guard dog so I was glad his house wasn't closer to the road or he might have chased after us.

We walked past his house a short distance before turning around on that gravel road and walking towards the dam. We could see some people fishing but Mr. Gilbert said we didn't have enough time to go there.

He said, "We have to get back to the school and wash up and if we don't hurry, we will be late for supper. I'm sure you boys wouldn't want to explain to Sister Superior why you kept her waiting."

That was a scary thought so we picked up the pace and walked faster. After all, we didn't want to walk into the dining room and have to explain ourselves to a wicked nun.

As we walked Ernest told us, "There was a grass fire around this area last spring. Someone was burning garbage, and the wind spread the flames to the surrounding dry grass and it got away. Some of the houses along the valley were evacuated until they got the fire under control. The river is a constant threat at this time of the year too because of all the snow that's melting in the hills."

My thoughts turned to my dad. What was his life like when he attended school here? Did he go for walks like this or did he just have to do hard work for the school? Dad was a hard worker, so he must have learned it somewhere. The only place I could think of was here at school.

I thought about it for a while and decided to ask him where he learned to work so hard the next time, I saw him.

I looked ahead and saw a few boys arriving at the school.

We would have to hurry before the whistle blew for supper. The air was filled with the smell of food cooking in the kitchen as we walked past the girls' side of the building.

Before supper, Mr. Dennis was watching the hockey game. He had the TV doors partially open, just wide enough so he could see what was happening.

I was hungry, but I also wanted to watch the game. It seemed like an eternity before the bell rang for us to file into the dining room.

Today's menu consisted of boiled eggs, mashed potatoes, vegetables, and pudding for dessert. I was hungry, so I was happy Sister Superior didn't remind us of all the starving children in Africa.

As we ate, our conversation turned to the "field day" that was quickly approaching.

I asked Ernest, "What happens on field day?"

"You have to compete in different events such as high jumping, broad jumping, ball throwing, 50-yard dash, 100-yard dash and relay races. You get coloured ribbons for placing first, second, or third. There are no classes that day, and we have a lot of fun."

Chapter 9 - Reminiscing About Home

The days were getting longer, and the weather had warmed up to the point we no longer needed parkas, toques, or mitts.

One day, Mr. Dennis told us to gather all the skates and hockey equipment in the dressing room so he could put them into storage. By now, the rink boards had been taken down and hauled away and the playground looked so different.

During our spare time, we were often involved in playing scrub at one of the ball diamonds. Organized sports were a big thing at Marieval.

I was walking around the playground when I noticed a track-and-field area with fresh white powder on it. More sand was in the high jump pit. I watched several boys jumping over a pole that was constantly being raised one inch at a time. According to the rules, you were given three chances to jump over the pole. If you were successful in clearing the pole, you waited for them to raise it another inch before attempting it again.

When the game started over, I decided to join them. I was able to clear the bar at two and a half feet, but when the pole was raised to three feet, I couldn't jump any higher.

Norman and Ernest were good at it; they could easily clear the bar at that height. They were both one year older than me, so that made a difference when it came to sports. They were good at most of the events in track-and-field, so I knew they were going to be hard to beat on field day.

I marvelled at some of the senior boys who could clear the bar that was over my head. There were different jumping styles. I remember one called the western roll.

During this particular jumping style, a competitor would throw one leg over the bar while rolling his body and pulling his other leg over the top. Some of the boys like Froggy had perfected this style and were fun to watch.

Another style was called scissors. It was my favourite way of jumping because it was simple. I learned this style by slowly stepping over the bar with my left leg followed by my right one.

When the bar got higher, I had to pick up more speed to clear the bar. As I flew through the air my legs made a scissors motion. I tried the western roll a couple of times, but I kept knocking the bar over with my knee, so I stayed with a scissors style.

As the days passed, I found myself thinking more and more about going home. I reminisced about all the fun things I used to do at home and tried to imagine what I would be doing if I was at home.

Maybe I could borrow one of Uncle Gordon's horses and ride around the reserve. I thought it over some more and concluded he probably wouldn't lend me one of his horses because he used them for work, but it wouldn't hurt to ask.

Back in those days, there were still quite a few families on White Bear who owned horses. Maybe someone would let me ride one of them.

With each passing day, my excitement grew. I found it difficult to go to bed at eight o'clock because it was still daylight outside. I thought of Mom and Dad. I thought of our grandparents, and I thought of my younger brother, Oranges. I wondered what they were all doing?

Oranges probably stayed up later than we did because back home we didn't have to come inside until it was getting dark. Oh, how I missed being at home.

The day of our track-and-field meet finally arrived. We didn't have any classes that day. The purpose of the field day was to meet and have fun while getting the students to be actively involved in track and field events.

We were called out on the playground then divided into smaller groups according to our grades.

Ms. Sedeski had a clipboard and called out our names as she took attendance and made sure everyone from our grade was present.

When she called Walter Grant, I raised my hand, even though it wasn't my name. Our teacher had called me that name for so long that it was now considered to be my name.

After ensuring everyone was present, she shared some of the rules with us. First of all, athletes were only allowed to compete in a maximum of six events. They should not register in events occurring at or near the same time, and spikes were not allowed during the competitions.

Athletes would be given three chances while competing at a certain event and only the top three competitors would be awarded ribbons. They would also qualify for the Provincial Finals in Broadview at a later date.

She brought us to a sandpit and explained the rules for this event, which was the standing broad jump.

We had to stand on a board with our toes behind the line and jump as far as we could. But only our farthest jump was recorded on Ms. Sedeski's clipboard.

I didn't get a ribbon for this event, but I smiled when she pinned a red ribbon on Blackie's shirt, a blue ribbon on Norman's shirt and a white ribbon on Ernest's shirt. That meant they came in first, second and third respectively.

We stayed at the same sandpit for our next event which was the running broad jump. Once again, we were given three chances to see how far we could jump into the sandpit.

A few of us stepped over the line as we jumped, so that one didn't count. Only two of my jumps counted, but I couldn't compete against Norman, Ernest and some of my other classmates as they were bigger and older than me.

I didn't do any better at the softball throw. I tried my best but came up short when they measured my farthest throw.

Many of my classmates received one or two ribbons for their efforts. Blackie, Ernest, and Norman received the most ribbons for many of the events; those ribbons sure looked good on them.

More ribbons were added to their collection when we went to the high jump pit and the track for some races.

At the end of our field day, the Principal Mr. Lang called out the names of the winners and said these students would be going to Broadview to represent Marieval at another track-and-field meet.

"Congratulations! I'm proud that you will be going to the provincials next week to represent Marieval! I'm confident each of you is going to do well against the athletes from other schools across the province."

Both Norman and Ernest were excited when their names were called, but I could tell they pitied me when my name wasn't on the list.

On Friday, quite a few students boarded a big yellow bus and left for the field day at Broadview.

Those who didn't make the trip were excused from school to go swimming at a nearby beach.

I looked forward to swimming and paddling around in the water near the shore. I also wanted to build some castles in the sand or collect seashells near the shore.

Mr. Gilbert said, "To avoid the boats that go sailing by, you need to stay inside the area marked off with coloured buoys." Although this was a good safety tip, most of us didn't know how to swim, so there was little chance we would venture out that deep into the water. But it was a good day for a swim; it was hot and the cool water felt good.

At noon hour our supervisor instructed some senior boys to build a fire for a wiener roast. It was fun roasting wieners and marshmallows over an open fire and it reminded me of the times we went camping at home. For an added treat our supervisor handed out bottles of pop.

We headed back to the school at four o'clock and waited anxiously for the students to return from Broadview.

When they arrived, they were excited as they showed off their ribbons and told the rest of us how much fun they had at the track-and-field meet. It sounded like I missed out on an awesome day, and I promised to try harder next year.

Norman asked. "What did you do while we were gone?"

I told him about our trip to the beach. "I went into the water up to my neck, and built a really big castle in the sand."

He shared about his day and told me there were a lot of students who attended the track-and-field meet. He proudly showed me two ribbons he'd won and said, "I'm going to show these ribbons to Mom and Dad when we go home for the holidays. They're going to be so proud!"

"What did you have for lunch?" I asked.

"We had a huge barbecue. I ate two hamburgers and had a grape pop to drink. I could have had more, but I still had to compete in some events and didn't want to stuff myself."

I told him about our lunch. "We roasted wieners and marshmallows and I had an orange pop to drink."

Somehow there was no comparison between his lunch and mine. He had a nice barbequed lunch.

I had a hard time sleeping that night because it was still bright outside at eight o'clock.

What was everyone doing back home? Maybe they were sitting around the supper table while listening to some of Grandpa's stories or visiting with relatives who occasionally stopped in for soup and bannock.

During those times, they spoke our Assiniboine language. Although I didn't know what they were talking about, it was good to see them sitting there teasing one another.

Dad was a Cree from down east, so he didn't understand the Assiniboine language like our mom did. Maybe he understood a few words, but he wasn't a fluent speaker.

Sometimes when they talked in Assiniboine, I would ask Mom what they were talking about. There were times when she told me what they said, but other times she put her finger to her lips, which meant to be quiet.

I must have fallen asleep while I was thinking of being at home. The next thing I knew, the dorm lights were on, and Sister David was yelling at us to get up and make our beds.

A couple of boys wet their beds, so we waited for them to take their soiled sheets down to the laundry room.

When they returned, she scolded them for not using the washroom during the night.

I pitied them; their faces turned red with embarrassment. I'm sure if they knew they had to use the washroom, they would've done so. Who wets their bed on purpose?

They looked scared as they quickly made their beds in silence and we were relieved when Mr. Dennis came to take us down to the playroom.

Sister David was very mean, and it was always stressful whenever she was around, while Grandma Smoker was more lenient with the junior boys who wet their beds.

We sure missed her when she wasn't here to supervise us.

On Monday morning June 19th Ms. Sedeski looked at her desk calendar and told us our summer holidays were quickly approaching. She reminded us we still had to write some tests for our final report cards. However, it wasn't something to worry about because the tests were mainly a review of the things we learned since we started school last fall.

We spent the next few days reviewing phonics, spelling and arithmetic to make sure we were going to be ready to write our final tests.

By the end of the week, Ms. Sedeski smiled and said, "I know you've worked hard this week and I believe everyone will be passing their tests next week."

After breakfast, on Saturday Mr. Gilbert came into the playroom. "Good morning," he said. "We're going on a picnic today."

He put a box of swimming trunks in the middle of the room. "Find a pair that fits you and I'll mark your number on the inside."

Mine was a small black pair of trunks that already had my number from the time we went swimming a few days ago. They were easy to identify and they fit me perfectly.

One of the junior boys asked me, "Can you swim?"

"I can swim in water up to my neck, but that's as deep as I can go. But I'm good at doing the dog paddle."

I envied some senior boys who could swim in deep water. For most of us, if the water was deeper than our shoulders, we'd stand on our tiptoes and turn back to shore. I thought of the times we went swimming at Carlyle Lake and looked forward to swimming there again.

We were ordered to go outside and meet the supervisors. Along with the help of a few senior boys, they had picked up our picnic supplies from the dining room and loaded them into a big truck.

We climbed into the back of that green 5-ton truck and the junior boys were instructed to stay in the front. A big chain in the centre was used to keep the sides of the truck box together. It was the boundary for the junior boys like me.

The ride was bumpy and dusty as we made our way down a gravel road that twisted and turned along the valley.

Every time we slowed down to pass through a hamlet beside the lake, I would stand up to see if there was a beach there. But for some reason, we just kept on driving.

It was a long time before we heard the truck gearing down and turning toward a beach.

We parked near a store, and I was excited when we were directed to a changing room and allowed to go into the water. It was cold at first, but after I played around for a while, I got used to it. I showed off my dog-paddling skills and made sure I didn't go in too deep.

Several senior boys swam farther out and reached some coloured buoys that fenced off the swimming area, but that was too deep for me.

Not far from the beach there was a small store that was constantly busy with people buying treats on this hot day. It sold chips, pop, ice-cream cones and confections.

I watched Mr. Gilbert enter the store and come out with a cold bottle of orange pop.

"Sir, can I go to the store and spend my dollar?"

"Okay, but hurry up. We're going to be leaving soon."

I quickly looked around in the store, but the more I tried to hurry, the more I didn't know what to buy. Everything looked so good, but eventually, I bought a bag of potato chips and an ice-cold root beer. I gave my dollar to the clerk and he gave me some change, which I put into my pocket without counting.

When I came out of the store, Norman and Ernest noticed me right away. They asked for some of my chips or a sip of my pop. Before I knew it, I had an empty pop bottle and an empty bag of chips. It was nice to see them smile when I shared my treats with them.

We rarely had an opportunity to buy something from a convenience store, and I knew they would have gladly shared with me if they had money to spend. So, my dollar went a long way and brought happiness to three lonely boys.

After we all changed out of our wet swimming trunks, we climbed back into the truck and headed down the road.

The supervisors rode in the cab of the truck, and we heard a radio playing every time they opened one of their doors.

We didn't mind the dusty, bumpy ride in the back of the truck because we were going for a wiener roast, and it was nice to get away from the school for a day.

While standing up and feeling the wind blowing on my face, I glanced at some people who were strolling down the road. They ignored us when they noticed it was a truckload of Indians going by.

I wondered what they thought because it wasn't every day, they witnessed such a sight.

An older boy said, "Sit down or you'll cook your name."

I wasn't sure what he meant, but I think he wanted me to sit down so I wouldn't embarrass him.

Indians commonly rode in the back of pickup trucks back then, and people stared and laughed at them for doing so.

I sat down so the rest of the boys didn't get upset with me for embarrassing them.

After we travelled a few miles down that gravel road, we could hear the truck gearing down before we turned onto a narrow trail. We parked in a ravine that was going to be our campsite. It was nestled among some trees and concealed from passing traffic. We found a perfect spot for our picnic.

We climbed out of the truck wondering what we were going to do next.

Then Mr. Dennis pulled out a white ball of string and gave us all a three-foot piece of it for making bows.

"If you don't have a pocket knife, team up with someone who does. Listen to the sound of my whistle at five o'clock. That will signal it's time for our wiener roast."

A few senior boys stayed at the campsite to cut firewood and help the supervisors unload the truck. It contained two large folding tables, a milk can full of juice, and some food for our picnic. The food looked so good and I wished we could have our wiener roast right away.

I wasn't going to miss the sound of our supervisor's whistle calling us back to our campsite.

Ernest, Norman, and I stayed together as we looked through the bush to find a grove of ash trees for our bows. Ash trees could bend without breaking and send arrows flying farther than bows made from any other species of trees. It didn't take long to find some ash trees. We looked them over to find ones with the right size branches for making sturdy bows.

After we finished making our bows, we searched for white willows to make our arrows. They had to be nice and straight without any curves or bends in them so they would fly straight toward a target.

Two of the bows and arrows the other boys made stood out for me. The first one that caught my eye was John's bow. It was fancy looking and made from an ash tree. His arrows were long and straight; some boys called them jungle arrows.

The other bow belonged to Ning-Ning. It was small but sturdy, and it could send arrows flying a great distance. It could have belonged to Robin Hood. Both Ning-Ning and John had perfected the art of making bows and arrows.

After we put together our weapons, Mr. Gilbert suggested we form two teams with John and Nin-Ning as captains. We were given a choice of which team we wanted to be on, so Norman, Ernest, and I chose to be on John's team.

Ning-Ning also had his little band of followers like Robin Hood and his merry men. Now we were going to have a mock war game. Each team had to build a fort and have a strategy for taking prisoners and capturing the enemy's fort.

John spoke, with excitement in his voice, as he shared his strategy for winning the war. He said, "We'll build our fort in this grove of trees. Ernest, Norman, and Walter will guard it and the rest of you will come with me as warriors."

As he spoke, he drew some diagrams in the dirt so we could see who was going to capture Ning-Ning and his fort.

I had a blast helping to build our fort while watching out for enemy warriors.

John said, "I'll be back in a little while to check on you and make sure Ning-Ning doesn't capture our fort. Whistle twice if you get into trouble. But don't whistle for nothing."

We played that adventurous game until we heard Mr. Gilbert blow his whistle. We knew it was time to return to our camp for our wiener roast.

In all of the excitement, I had forgotten how hungry I was until we got back to our camp and saw all that food laid out on a table. Along with the food, there were some sticks for roasting our wieners and marshmallows.

We lined up for the food a senior boy was handing out on paper plates.

After he filled our plates, he gave us a paper cup and told us, "Help yourselves for some juice at the end of the table."

These wiener roasts were more enjoyable than our meals in the dining room because we didn't have to pray before we ate and we didn't have to finish eating our meal in silence.

I ate one of my wieners raw because I remembered eating them that way back home when we went to Carlyle with Mom and Dad. I carefully selected a stick with a good-sized fork so I could roast a couple of wieners at the same time.

Standing by the fire and watching my wieners roast until they were done to perfection was entertaining. They tasted good, and after wolfing down my hotdogs, I was getting full.

One of my friends, Wesley left a wiener roasting on a stick while he went to refill his cup with juice.

When he returned, his wiener was burnt and shrivelled up. He smiled as he picked it up and said, "Mmm, just the way I like it."

After everyone had their fill of hot dogs, Mr. Gilbert pulled out a few bags of marshmallows and said, "Now for dessert, we are going to roast marshmallows."

Watching some boys trying to blow out a small fire on their marshmallows or someone trying to eat a marshmallow that was still hot on the inside was amusing.

We sat around the fire until the sun was going down and it was time to go back to the school.

Later that evening, we were told to get ready for our weekly shower.

I wasn't paying attention to what I was doing and took my time getting into the shower. There was a lot of steam in there and it was difficult for me to see where I was going.

Before I realized what was happening, a supervisor grabbed me and pulled me under a faucet.

He held a bar of soap in one hand and a face cloth in the other as he lathered me all over with that bar of soap. Soap was running down my forehead and getting into my eyes, making it all the more difficult to move around on that slippery floor.

I tried to tell him I could wash, but he didn't listen to me. I didn't mind when he washed my neck and upper torso, but when he stuck his hand inside my shorts, I tried to move away from him. This upset him and he yelled at me.

He jerked me roughly up against his hairy chest. He turned me around. His crotch rubbing against my back felt gross. A strong body odour came from under his hairy armpits, and I was happy when he finished washing me as the water was turning cold.

I was going to get out of the shower when he said, "Stand under the cold water and rinse that soap out of your hair".

By the time I was done, I was shaking like a leaf. What had occurred in the shower traumatized me and I wanted to be as far away from that supervisor and this place as possible. I wanted to go home where I would be safe.

I looked forward to seeing Grandma Smoker again, but when we walked into our dorm Sister David was sitting in Grandma Smoker's chair.

"Get ready for bed and make it quick," she said.

A large set of keys dangled from the side of this grumpy-looking nun's habit. I tried not to look at her because the senior boys said she used her keys to hit them on the head when she got upset.

We quickly changed into our pyjamas and brushed our teeth, then sister David told us to kneel by our beds while she prayed with her rosary.

After she prayed for an eternity, she yelled at us to climb into bed and turned out the lights for the night.

Early the next morning, we put on our grey pants, white shirts, and oxford shoes we found at the foot of our beds.

After everyone was dressed, we lined up by the exit door and waited patiently for a supervisor to come for us.

When we arrived, downstairs Mr. Dennis told everyone to meet him on the sidewalk near our playroom entrance. From there we marched in two rows to the church.

I was surprised when there were no catechism classes.

One of the nuns directed us to the front pews for the Mass.

I looked around the church and near the front, there were some lit candles in coloured glass containers. There were rows upon rows of different coloured ones, and some of them were lit while others were not.

When the Mass started, I watched the altar boys as they moved to different parts of the chancel and somehow, they always knew exactly where to be when Father Carriere needed them for something.

During the sermon, I tried my best to listen to what the priest was saying, but he talked for such a long time, I started to doze off. I heard giggling coming from behind me when my head started to bob around. I couldn't help it, and before long, my drowsiness got the best of me. I must've dozed off because I felt a sharp pain in my right ear as one of the nuns twisted my ear and scolded me for falling asleep. That did the trick; I was wide awake for the rest of the service.

Later that afternoon, Ernest said, "Our summer holidays will be starting soon."

The thought of going home was exciting. As we sat on a bench near the junior boys' ball diamond, Ernest, Norman, and I talked about some of the fun things we wanted to do during the summer. We smiled as we took turns sharing.

Ernest said, "I want to go to Carlyle and hang out in town for a day."

Norman replied, "I want to explore some new trails near our grandparents' place."

When it was my turn, there were so many things I wanted to do that I didn't know where to begin. Finally, after thinking about it for a while, I said, "I want to go for a swim at the lake. I also want to go into the Hotel Beach store for pop, ice-cream cones, and chips.

They agreed that was something to look forward to doing, and although we were miles from home, we kept one another company. Being together helped combat the loneliness we felt from being stuck here.

After supper, Mr. Dennis informed us some senior boys were going to the gym for a dance. He called out the numbers for the boys who would be attending, but my number wasn't on the list. That was okay with me because I didn't care about dancing. I felt more comfortable playing games in the playroom and watching television.

When our favourite show *Bonanza* started, I forgot about my loneliness and my eyes were glued to the television set.

During this episode, Little Joe kept bugging his older brother, Hoss and laughed at him when he got upset. Hoss looked frustrated and pretended to be mad, but I don't think he was mad at Little Joe.

When the show was over, we lined up and went to the junior boys' dorm. It was good to see Grandma Smoker sitting there waiting for us. She wasn't as mean as the nuns and didn't make us kneel by our beds while she said long-winded prayers with her rosary. She let us read our comics or visit one another before she turned out the lights.

Usually, it didn't take me long to fall asleep, but tonight I was restless. As I lay in bed, my thoughts turned to the time Dad told us our late grandmother, Nancy Smoker, came from the Kahkewistahaw reserve. Our dorm supervisor had the same last name, so maybe she was related to us.

The surname Smoker was not a common name near Marieval. If our grandmother Nancy Smoker hadn't married our grandfather, Alexander, then Smoker would have been our last name too.

I had so many unanswered questions, yet I had to keep them to myself. If word got out that Norman and I were related to our dorm supervisor, I'm sure the news would spread like wildfire. It might even cost Grandma Smoker her job. I fell asleep wondering about our family and trying to sort things out. Were we related or not?

On Monday morning, June 26th, when we returned to class, Ms. Sedeski informed us we were going to be writing tests for our final report cards.

The questions in arithmetic started easy, but they quickly progressed to more difficult ones. By the end of the test, I was starting to second guess myself.

The reading and spelling tests were easier to handle. I felt more confident about these subjects.

For the rest of the week, we cleaned out our desks and took down our artwork from the windows.

Ms. Sedeski said, "Keep your scribblers and the art you want to take home."

"Norman, are you going to keep your art to show Mom and Dad?"

He showed me a couple of pictures where our younger brother, Oranges, was playing. "I want to give these pictures to Mom so she can show them to Grandma and Grandpa."

Ernest said he was going to take home a couple of his pictures to share with our grandparents.

Friday was our last day of school, and Ms. Sedeski said, "Today you're going to receive your report cards. I'm so proud of your accomplishments throughout the school year."

She mentioned some of the highlights that stood out for her. One of them was the Christmas concert and the square-dance we performed. She also informed us her husband had enjoyed supervising us this year. This came as a surprise to us because we didn't know her husband was a supervisor!

After she finished speaking, she wiped away a tear from her eye. She quickly changed the subject and began handing out our report cards.

When I received mine, I glanced toward the back of my report card. I had passed into Grade-two!

This year, everyone passed their grade and we would all be going into Grade-two next year.

Ms. Sedeski told us to enjoy our summer holidays before dismissing us one final time.

We returned to our playroom and said farewell to the day scholars. After all, we wouldn't be seeing them again until next September. We were all in a festive mood.

Some of the students who lived across the creek or within walking distance from the school went home as soon as we were dismissed. They were lucky. Their summer holidays had already started, but we would have to wait until the school arranged a ride home for us or someone picked us up.

Throughout the day, many of the parents or caregivers stopped by to pick up their children.

By evening, there were only a few of us left at the school. We were excited when Father Carriere informed us he made arrangements for the White Bear students to be transported as far as Kennedy tomorrow. From there, someone from the reserve would pick us up.

I could hardly believe what was happening. We were going home tomorrow!

That night, we were allowed to stay up and watch TV until ten o'clock.

Mr. Dennis told us, "Everyone will be sleeping in the senior boys' dorm tonight."

Although I was grateful for staying up late, I was a little disappointed about not seeing Grandma Smoker one final time before we started our holidays.

After the lights were turned out in the dorm, I thought of our summer holidays ahead. I wanted to sleep in a tent again. I looked forward to hanging out with my brothers and checking out old wagon trails back home. I also relished the idea of going to Carlyle and watching a movie in the show hall. I wanted to go swimming at the lake; but most of all, I wanted to see our family again.

My excitement about going home woke me early the next morning before the lights came on. I wanted to go wake up Norman and tell him to get up.

I tiptoed to the washroom and noticed someone going in there. It was Norman.

He smiled and said, "We're going home today!"

"I know it's going be great to leave this hell hole behind and spend the rest of our summer at home."

We went back to our beds while we waited for the lights to come on. It was daylight at seven-thirty a.m. when the lights finally came on and most of us were already awake.

Sister David came to the dorm to give us a change of clothes. She asked me, "Do you want to wear the shoes you came to school with or do you prefer running shoes?"

I looked at the girl's shoes in her hand and pointed to the black-and-white runners she held in the other hand.

She handed me the new canvas running shoes and tossed Shirley's old shoes in the garbage. Now, I wouldn't have to go home wearing shoes with my two toes sticking out.

When we were in the dining room for breakfast, I was surprised there were only a few of us left at school. But we still had to pray before we ate and I didn't feel hungry at all.

After we finished eating breakfast Sister Superior prayed with us and wished us a safe journey home.

As we lined up to leave the dining room, Shirley smiled and waved at us.

When we were back in our playroom, we sat quietly on the benches wondering what was going to happen next.

Then, we heard footsteps coming down the stairs. Father Carriere opened our playroom door. "Meet me in front of the parlour," he said.

From there, he directed us to the parking lot where a small bus was waiting to take us to Kennedy. We had waited for this special day for nine months. Finally, we were leaving this awful school behind for the summer.

When we arrived at the town hall in Kennedy, I asked Norman and Ernest, "Is there a washroom around?"

They both said they didn't think there was one inside the building. It looked like I would have to wait until we got to Kenosee. There was a picnic site near the #9 highway but I didn't think I could wait that long. So, there I was in dire need of relieving myself, and not knowing what to do.

About that time, Veronica noticed me squirming around. "What's wrong?" she asked.

"I need to use the washroom."

She smiled and pointed to a large, brown door that said, 'MEN.' She told me I could use that one, so I thanked her and went racing to the washroom that had three large urinals along the wall.

Oh, what a relief. Shortly after that Norman and Ernest came racing in to use the washroom.

Ernest said, "Hurry up. Our ride will be coming soon."

Sure enough, shortly after someone showed up and told us to climb into his van because he was hired to give us a ride home. It was exciting knowing we were starting the final leg of our journey home. There were only a few of us in the van but everyone looked so happy.

As we pulled out of Kennedy, I noticed the rodeo grounds and recalled a time we watched Dad ride at a rodeo there.

Many cowboys were riding and Dad was one of them, along with another rider called Edward from White Bear. Dad was a good rider and managed to stay on a bucking bronc for eight seconds. He smiled and waved at the crowd after a pickup rider helped him off a wild bucking horse.

Edward got on a bull but didn't make it for eight seconds. He got bucked off before the buzzer sounded and he jumped onto the corral chute as the bull chased him. The clowns distracted the bull long enough for him to make a getaway.

As we drove by Kenosee Provincial Park, I noticed how green the trees were with wildlife everywhere. Ducks and geese were swimming in the lake while a doe with her two spotted fawns walked slowly into the bush.

Shortly after, I saw a green sign that said, "Welcome to White Bear Reserve."

When we arrived at Squaw Point, we stopped to let Veronica off and Ernest saw some cars parked across the road, "Hey look there's a Kentucky Fried Chicken stand that's open. I wonder if Grandma will want to come and buy some chicken for Grandpa later? I'm going to ask her."

It was exciting to be home with our summer holidays just beginning. This was a very good day for all of us including our siblings, parents and Grandparents.

Chapter 10 - Endless Days of Summer

When we pulled up in front of our grandparents' house, Mom and Dad were standing in the yard waiting for us.

They smiled and thanked the driver for bringing us home.

Mom hugged us for a long time and she had tears in her eyes, so I asked her, "What's wrong, Mom?"

She said, "Nothing, I'm just so happy to see you."

Oranges was peeking at us from around the corner of the house. Somehow, we all felt shy and unsure of what to do, so Mom told us to take our belongings into the house.

Shirley and Ernest took their report cards and papers into our grandparents' house while Norman and I took our report cards and artwork into the log shack next door.

Mom told us to go and visit our grandparents because they were waiting to see us.

Grandma moved around in the kitchen making lunch. "Oh, it's so nice to see you, again! I'm happy you're home for the summer!"

Grandpa sat in his stuffed armchair drinking tea. He smiled, looking us up and down before asking, "How high can you count?"

We both said we could count to a hundred. However, I wasn't sure if I could count to a hundred, so I was glad he didn't ask me to count for him. By now, their house was getting hot from the wood stove, so Norman told Grandpa he wanted to go and play outside.

He smiled and said, "Okay, but let your mom know where you're going."

We promised we would do that and headed next door to be with our parents.

Mom said, "Later I'm going to make soup and bannock. I'll let you know when it's ready."

We spent the rest of the day exploring trails leading down to *the hollow* and another one leading to a slough where we watched some ducks and geese swimming around.

We went home and told Dad about the geese and ducks in the slough so, he borrowed Grandpa's double-barrel 12-gauge shotgun and invited us to come with him.

We quietly followed him until he said, "Wait here while I go ahead. I'm going to sneak up on them"

He disappeared into the bulrushes. After he was gone for twenty minutes, I asked Norman, "Has he shot at them yet?"

Norman was about to answer when we heard a loud boom followed by a second shot, both of them sounding like cannons going off.

We waited for Dad to return and we were surprised when he had four ducks but wasn't wet from the slough water.

I asked, "How did you get the ducks out of the water without getting wet?"

He said, "Snap is a good retriever. He brought them to the shore for me."

I patted Snap, "You're a good dog," I told him.

When we returned home, Dad dropped off Grandpa's shotgun and gave him two ducks for letting him use it.

Our grandparents were grateful for the ducks and thanked Dad for dropping them off.

Grandma said, "Oh, this makes me so happy. I've been wishing for duck soup."

That afternoon, Mom plucked and singed the ducks and put them in a pot on the stove.

We hadn't eaten duck soup for nearly a year. The aroma of those two ducks cooking, a smell I loved, filled our house.

Mom also made some fry bread to go with the duck soup, and I stuffed myself until I could barely move. It was great to taste Mom's cooking again.

That summer, Dad found a lot of work as a hired hand for neighbouring farmers. We moved around a lot, living on farms near Kipling, Kennedy, Wawota, and Carlyle.

When Dad couldn't find work, we stayed in a large white canvas tent in the bush while he cut pickets to sell to local farmers. He would spend hours in the bush from daybreak to sundown, cutting and peeling the bark off his pickets.

Sometimes he would receive an order for the posts to be soaked in bluestone so they wouldn't rot in the ground. It was more work for him, but they sold for more money.

When he was paid for his pickets, we drove into town for gas, groceries, and treats.

At times, Mom and Dad would take us to go and visit with our relatives down east. For a while, we camped in a tent close to Uncle Willie's house near Heart Hill.

Our cousins—Jeff, Burl, and Eugene—often came to hang out with us when we stayed in the bush near their place.

Sometimes when Dad got paid, both of our parents would sit in the bar in Carlyle. There were quite a few people who drank, so it wasn't hard for them to find a party.

Alcoholism plagued our community, and it was especially noticeable in town on certain days of the month.

Many of our relatives bought wine and went across the railroad tracks to drink.

When they returned, you could see them staggering down the street where an R.C.M.P. paddy wagon waited for them.

The police cruised around the bar and stopped vehicles as they were leaving town. To avoid getting stopped by the police, many impaired drivers used the back roads.

Dad knew the back roads quite well, so we always managed to make it home without getting pulled over.

Others weren't so lucky, and they got charged with impaired driving.

During the summer when we stayed in the log shack beside our grandparents' place, they always made sure our parents stayed sober. Those were happy times.

We went to the bush to explore new trails or make bows and arrows to go hunting with. We never killed anything on any of our adventures, but we had a lot of fun making our toys in the bush.

Norman was good at making slingshots, so constructing them became one of our favourite pastimes during the long lazy days of summer.

Sometimes, Mom would go berry picking with Grandma and some of our extended family members. They tied pails around their necks to free up their hands for picking. When they discovered a good berry patch, it was like finding a gold mine. Everyone was happy because it didn't take them long to fill up their berry containers.

Grandma would often preserve saskatoons, raspberries, and rhubarb for the winter. She also made jam out of some of those berries, and it sure tasted good on toast. She would occasionally take some berries to the lake to sell to the cottagers. She never had a problem selling her berries.

Some people would watch us coming their way and wave their money in the air so we could see them better. It reminded me of an ice-cream truck where people waited patiently for their turn.

I enjoyed those trips to the lake because it meant going into the *Hotel Beach* store for ice cream, chips, and pop.

When we went swimming, Grandma would tell us to spread a blanket on the ground so we would have a dry place to rest when we came out of the water.

Some of the better swimmers would dive off a tower that was placed farther out in the water. It was too deep for us, but we did have a large raft to jump off. It was anchored closer to the shore and it was always in use by the younger boys and girls.

We attended a few pow-wows that summer because Dad had a nice outfit and liked to dance.

When he prepared his regalia for an upcoming pow-wow, I watched him preen his eagle feathers and his two white ostrich feathers over a boiling kettle of water.

He was easy to spot among the dancers because of the white feathers on the top of his roach.

Although I didn't know how to sing or dance, something in the drumbeat made me feel good about being an Indian.

A few times, I thought of what we were learning at Marieval about being pagans and worshipping the devil. But I knew it wasn't wrong to attend these pow-wows. It wasn't wrong to be an Indian.

The endless days of summer dragged on. Without a schedule to follow, we enjoyed everything that came our way. We were allowed to stay up until dark and probably would have stayed up longer, but we didn't have electricity. The only lights we had were from a coal oil lamp.

We often woke up to the sound of Mom humming a song as she made breakfast over a hot wood stove. The smell of the wood smoke and from her cooking permeated our one-room log shack.

When our breakfast was ready, she would tell us to wash our hands and faces in a basin filled with fresh rainwater before we sat down to eat.

Dad would sit at the table listening to country songs like "Your Cheatin' Heart" by Hank Williams from a little transistor radio. Another one of his favourite singers was Johnny Cash, who was new to the music industry.

We didn't have a TV, but there was always music playing in our home, whether it was coming from the radio or Dad singing pow-wow songs.

Anytime we wanted to do something, we merely had to ask Mom for permission. She would say, "Go ahead, but make sure you look after Oranges."

Our little brother was two years younger than me, and he wanted to follow us wherever we went. Sometimes he was a bit of a pain, but most of the time, it was fun having him tag along with us.

One day I sat with Grandma in the shade of the house as she smashed chokecherries and made patties out of them. She would place chokecherries on a large flat rock and crush them with a smaller flat one.

When she had crushed enough of them, she made them into patties and put them on an outdoor table Grandpa made for her to dry them in the hot sun. It was constructed out of four posts nailed to a sheet of plywood and high enough so the dogs couldn't get at her patties but low enough for Grandma to reach them.

One night when Grandma was going to use the outhouse before going to bed, she heard a munching sound coming from her chokecherry drying table.

She shone her flashlight in that direction and saw some big eyes looking back at her. She was frightened out of her wits, so she called Grandpa to the door.

He carried his lantern out with him and discovered his horses were out of the corral and munching on Grandma's crushed chokecherries. The drying table was just the right height for them to have a feast.

Grandpa had a good laugh over it, but Grandma didn't find it funny for the longest time. Usually, when the patties were dry, she had Grandpa put them in the cellar. Her latest batch was in the process of drying when Grandpa's horses got into them.

Other times, I helped Grandpa carry potatoes, turnips, radishes, carrots, onions, and corn from his garden to store in the cellar. He took a lot of pride in his garden and even made a scarecrow to keep the predators away. But that didn't always work for the human ones.

One-time Grandpa asked me to come with him to check on his garden. As we climbed through the barbed wire fence, he discovered some little tracks leading to his radishes and carrots. He looked at the discarded radish and carrot tops then looked down at my shoes.

"A little person has been eating my vegetables. I wonder who that could have been."

Grandpa sure had a way of making a little person feel guilty to the point of squirming around.

I was the only little person for miles around who wore a small size-six shoe; I think he knew it was me. I forgot to cover my tracks and learned a valuable lesson that day.

As the summer wore on, I felt sorry for Shirley and her younger siblings because their mom, Mariah, passed away.

This came as quite a shock to everyone because she was young and no one knew she was sick. She was living with our uncle Ernie at the time.

My parents attended her wake and funeral, but Shirley and her siblings stayed at Grandma's place because children were not allowed to view the bodies of dead people.

The funeral procession passed by our grandparents' home on its way to the Catholic cemetery above our place.

I was surprised when Ernest didn't cry or talk about his mom. If it was me, I would've been devastated.

Grandma explained we all have different ways of dealing with bad things that come our way, and this was his way of dealing with his mom's death.

I was too young to know about death, but I was curious to know why she passed away.

After the funeral, I asked Mom, "What happened to Auntie Mariah?"

She said, "Auntie Mariah died from alcohol poisoning. That's what happens when people drink too much. In other words, she got sick and died in her sleep."

I felt sorry for my cousins because they would have to grow up without a mom. To make matters worse, their dad, Uncle Ernie, liked to party, so he spent a lot of time in jail. But they were fortunate to have our grandparents to give them a good home.

As the days passed, I noticed they were getting shorter and the leaves on the trees were turning colours. There was no shortage of work for Dad because the harvest season had just started. But the fall season also meant our holidays were coming to an end.

Mom used her family allowance to buy us new clothes for school. But Oranges felt left out, so she bought him a cap gun, complete with a few rolls of caps and a gun holster.

When we came out of the store, his smile beamed from ear to ear. He could hardly wait to go home and play with his new gun.

We saw some of our friends and relatives in Carlyle.

They were also getting new clothes for starting school.

It was a sad day for all of us on Sunday, September 3rd when it was time to return to Marieval. We said farewell to our grandparents and told them we would write to let them know how we were doing.

Grandma said, "You be sure to do that. My mailbox is #248 in Carlyle." She hugged us and told Shirley to look after Faye at school.

Our younger cousin Faye turned six years old so she would be going into grade-one this year.

Mom and Dad drove us to the band office where a van was waiting to take us back to Marieval.

Norman and I were crying when we stepped into the van because we knew we weren't going to be seeing our family again for a very long time.

The smell of the exhaust in the back of the van where we were riding made me feel nauseous. By the time we got to Broadview, I felt like throwing up.

Annie asked the driver if he could stop so we could use the washroom. But it was too late; before I could get out of the van, I threw up on the floor.

I went racing into the washroom where I threw up some more. I was happy to see a sink in the washroom so I could wash my face and clean myself up. I looked in the mirror and noticed how pale I looked. I sure didn't feel well and wasn't looking forward to the rest of the ride to Marieval. I wasn't sure if I was going to be able to clean up my mess without getting sick again.

When I returned to the van, I was relieved to see our driver returning with cleaning supplies.

Some of the other students took advantage of our short break by going into the service station and buying chips, pop, and assorted candies.

I stayed by the van because I didn't feel like eating or drinking anything. I felt too sick.

When Annie returned to the van, she volunteered to clean up the mess I made. Without complaining, she made sure the van was spotless. She also thought it would be a good idea if I rode in the front with the vent window open so I would have fresh air.

The ride from Broadview to Marieval was better after I moved to the front of the van and I could breathe in the fresh air instead of the exhaust fumes.

When we rounded the corner and drove past Mr. Leost's store, I wanted to cry because we were almost at the school, and we were going to be stuck here until our Christmas holidays. This meant days, weeks, and months of being mistreated and not being able to see Mom and Dad.

Some junior boys and girls started to cry when Marieval came into sight. The older boys and girls were quiet too, and I could tell they weren't very happy about being here.

After parking the van, our driver directed us to the parlour where someone would be waiting for us.

Sure enough, Father Carriere and Sister Superior came down the steps and told us to line up in two rows.

The girls followed Sister Superior to their playroom while Father Carriere led us to the boys' playroom. He called our supervisors and told them we were back from our holidays.

I didn't feel like doing anything, so I sat on a bench in our playroom and reflected on my life here.

My home was more than a hundred miles away. I wouldn't hear Grandpa's stories for a long time. I was stuck in this residential school where it was wrong to be an Indian.

In a little while, my name would be replaced by a number, and I would have to come running when they called it. The new clothes Mom bought for me would be taken away and replaced with a uniform. Any mention of my culture was forbidden, so I would have to be careful not to break this rule. After all, our pagan ways were considered to be the work of the devil, and I would be told to pray for my ancestors because they were probably burning in hell.

In a little while, we would be lining up to go to the dining room where our diet from the land would be replaced with processed food. Sister Superior would go over a list of the rules she would strictly enforce. She ruled the dining room with an iron fist and ensured we ate all the food we were given because some children were starving in Africa. We would have to be vigilant of the bell she carried because the sound of that bell meant silence. Any infraction of that rule meant we would be reprimanded in front of everyone.

There were rules for everything we did from the time we woke up in the morning until the time we went to bed at night. We were constantly being corrected for something we did or did not do. Our punishment came in many forms depending on the severity of our mistakes.

There were rules from the Bible, but they didn't call them rules. They called them commandments. There were ten of them, and we had to follow them if we wanted to go to heaven. We would be ordered to live our lives the way Christ lived his life in the Bible. If we fell asleep or talked in church, we would be disciplined.

Another thing I learned in this residential school was to watch out for bullies because of the lateral violence here. Some of the senior boys liked to pick on the younger ones and make them cry. This violence stemmed from the nuns, priests, and staff who hit the students with rulers, keys, and straps to vent their anger.

I lived in constant fear of making a mistake that was going to get me into trouble. I had to live a perfect life here. There was only one person who lived a perfect life on earth, and he was crucified. When he died on the cross, everyone was happy. I couldn't understand why Christians killed their god and celebrated it as a good thing.

I would long for the days of being at home where it wasn't wrong to be an Indian. I would miss Mom's home-cooked meals where I didn't have to wait for the sound of a bell to tell me I could start eating. I enjoyed our meals at home because they usually ended with Grandpa telling us interesting stories where there was a lesson to be learned.

During the winter we played a game where we tossed a rabbit's head into the air and asked it a question when it landed on the table. We could only ask it three questions much like the genie in the lamp, who only grants three wishes.

On New Year's Day, we welcomed visitors into our home where they stuffed themselves with nutritious food that came from the land. Our visitors were encouraged to have second helpings and no one left our grandparents' home hungry

Back home, no one talked about going to hell where a devil waited for us in a huge fire that burned forever.

Grandpa said we didn't commit sins. He called them "learning experiences," and each one was sacred because they taught us about life, and life is sacred. Grandpa was a very wise man and there were a lot of things the nuns and priests could learn from him.

Oh, I forgot. We were heathens and our ways were the work of the devil, but for some reason, I didn't believe Grandpa was going to hell when he died.

My thoughts were interrupted by a supervisor telling us he would be right back to go over the rules with us. I sat there quietly waiting for him to return, as I dealt with feelings of loneliness, abandonment, and culture shock.

This was a very sad time for us and it felt like there was no hope for tomorrow.

About the Author

Robert is from White Bear First Nations in SK. He lives on Whitecap Dakota First Nation near Saskatoon, SK. He is the founder of Kakakaway & Associates Consulting, an Indigenous organization that offers ceremonial teachings.

Robert completed his B.G.S. degree at UBC in 1992. He also completed several post-secondary diploma programs.

Robert attended Marieval Indian Residential School for six years. He shares his daily experiences and the hardships he faced inside the prison walls of this residential school. His story talks about a common theme in most residential schools: it was wrong to be an Indian.

More from the Publisher

NAPI CHILDREN'S BOOKS:

- Napi and the Rock
- Napi and the Bullberries
- Napi and the Wolves
- Napi and the Buffalo
- Napi and the Chickadees
- Napi and the Coyote
- Napi and the Elk
- Napi and the Gophers
- Napi and the Mice
- Napi and the Bobcat
- Napi and The Jump
- Napi: The Anthology
- … and many more

GRAPHIC NOVELS:
- UNeducation: A Residential School Graphic Novel
- Napi the Trixster: A Blackfoot Graphic Novel
- UNeducation 2: The Side of Society You Don't See on TV

COLLABORATIONS:
- Thunderbird Rising
- Young Water Protectors
- Mukwa & The Suitcase
- The Empowerment of Eahwahewi
- Descendants of Warriors
- Hello … Fruit Basket
- How The Earth Was Created
- I Am The Opioid Crisis
- My Ribbon Skirts
- The Secret of the Stars
- Aahksoyo'p Nootski Cookbook
- … and many many more

If you absolutely loved this book, please tell your friends, then find it on AMAZON.COM and leave a quick review. Your words help more than you may realize. Thanks so much. For bulk orders, and more Indigenous awesomeness, visit **eaglespeaker.com**

Manufactured by Amazon.ca
Bolton, ON